Vocational
EDUCATION
in Canada

Vocational
EDUCATION
in Canada

The Past, Present, and Future of Policy

ALISON TAYLOR

I S S U E S   I N   C A N A D A

OXFORD
UNIVERSITY PRESS

OXFORD
UNIVERSITY PRESS

Oxford University Press is a department of the University of Oxford.
It furthers the University's objective of excellence in research, scholarship,
and education by publishing worldwide. Oxford is a registered trade mark of
Oxford University Press in the UK and in certain other countries.

Published in Canada by
Oxford University Press
8 Sampson Mews, Suite 204,
Don Mills, Ontario M3C 0H5 Canada

www.oupcanada.com

Library and Archives Canada Cataloguing in Publication

Taylor, Alison, 1959–, author
Vocational education in Canada / Alison Taylor.

Includes bibliographical references and index.
ISBN 978-0-19-900998-5 (paperback)

1. Vocational education--Canada. I. Title.
LC1047.C2T39 2015   370.1130971   C2015-906977-7

Cover image: © iStock/sturti

Oxford University Press is committed to our environment.
This book is printed on Forest Stewardship Council® certified paper
and comes from responsible sources.

Printed and bound in Canada

1 2 3 4 — 19 18 17 16

MIX
Paper from
responsible sources
FSC® C004071

To my children, Kieran and Robyn

To my children, Koen and Robyn

Contents

Contents

Acknowledgements

Much of the apprenticeship research on which this book is based was collaborative. I would therefore like to acknowledge my co-investigator, Dr. Wolfgang Lehmann, on a study called "Tracking High School Apprentices," as well as Dr. Milosh Raykov and Dr. Zane Hamm who worked with us as post-doctoral researchers. Previous research on Ontario apprentices was undertaken with help from research assistant Bonnie Watt-Malcolm as part of the *Work and Lifelong Learning* (WALL) project (Dr. D.W. Livingstone, Principal Investigation). I would also like to thank research assistants Renate Kahlke, Laura Servage, and Robyn Taylor-Neu as well as Jen Rubio from Oxford University Press for their help in preparing this manuscript. I am grateful to the Social Sciences and Humanities Research Council (SSHRC) and to the Canadian Council on Learning (CCL) for funding my research on high school apprentices.

Chapter 1

Introduction

The expectation that education systems should prepare young people for work has long been the subject of discussion, both in international policy circles and around the dinner table. However, changes in the economy and in work over time have brought about changes in that expectation. For example, the idea that we live in a *knowledge economy* has resulted in different ideas about what levels and what kinds of skills are needed for twenty-first-century learners vis-à-vis popular ideas at the beginning of the twentieth century. Furthermore, the growing polarization of "good jobs" and "bad jobs," along with increasing average educational attainment, has shifted the emphasis from a singular focus on producing more skilled graduates to seeking a better match between graduates' skills and actual labour-market requirements. Changes in career and work structures have led to the idea that individuals must engage in lifelong learning. This in turn has led to increased emphasis on learning in the workplace and continuing professional development to promote worker adaptability.

This book contributes to the discussion about preparing youth for work by taking a critical look at what changes in the demand for labour and skills ("demand side" changes) mean for the expectations placed on schools, how schools have responded to these expectations over time, and how they should respond in the future. Although the following chapters focus on compulsory education in Canada, the themes have broader relevance, as many countries wrestle with the conundrum of how to develop their education systems in light of profound economic and social changes.

European countries, for example, are responding with policies that promote the massification of higher secondary education, the move to competency-based qualifications, and interest in lifelong learning and continuing vocational education and training (VET) (Méhaut, 2012). National differences in responses and strategies regarding general and vocational education are related to the extent to which vocational education is integrated into countries' education systems and whether the training system is inclusive or not. "Inclusion" refers to who is able to participate in VET, since social participation is increasingly seen as dependent on a successful transition into working life (Stolz & Gonon, 2012). For example, Sweden has an integrated and inclusive model with tightly interwoven general and vocational education that provides access to tertiary education (Méhaut, 2012). In contrast, countries with strong apprenticeship systems such as Germany and Switzerland tend to have more separate but inclusive general and vocational education systems. Finally, liberal-market countries such as the UK and Canada have a strong separation between general and vocational education, and value the latter less. Policy-makers in North America and Europe face challenges concerning movement between general and vocational education and struggle to balance the aims of providing education and training that has labour-market value while also allowing for access to higher education.

My Approach in This Book

Sociologists of education before me have observed that education has long been a site of struggle between different players over what kind of knowledge is valued, who controls this knowledge, and who has access to it. My own research supports these observations: specifically, this book's argument is informed by my analyses of secondary school reform, high school apprenticeship, streaming, and school choice. This book will contribute to existing dialogue by considering developments in vocational education over time and the underlying agendas behind these developments. In the following chapters, I also identify the shifting players and interests that are involved in discussions about education and the workplace. Further, I offer critiques of policies that perpetuate inequity while suggesting guiding principles for more socially just policies. Several core assumptions and concerns inform my thinking:

1. *The problems with neo-liberal policy and human capital theory.*
Neo-liberalism promotes individualism in the context of an institutional framework that supports a minimalist state, privatization, deregulation, free markets, and free trade (Harvey, 2005). Its forms of governance construct political subjects as entrepreneurial, enterprising, and innovative; individuals are encouraged to see themselves as active subjects responsible for enhancing their own well-being (Larner, 2000). This policy

approach has been evident in educational reform discourses that emphasize the need for individuals to be flexible and adaptable, to develop entrepreneurial skills, and to be lifelong learners. The North American VET system has been characterized as a market-oriented system with few institutional mechanisms to smooth the transitions for youth (Grubb, 2006), in contrast to more coordinated approaches in European countries such as Germany and Denmark.

North American approaches also posit that individuals who invest in their education and training will reap labour-market rewards. More generally, human capital theory, which gained currency in the 1960s, stresses the role of formal education in securing economic productivity (Becker, 1964). More recently, this emphasis has been reflected in the idea that the knowledge-based economy has resulted in a general upskilling of work, requiring higher levels of formal education.

But there are problems with this outlook. Critics point out that education is only one of multiple influences on economic growth (Grubb, 2006). Further, while educational attainment has continued to increase since the early 1970s, average incomes have stagnated, unemployment rates have increased, and the underemployment of highly schooled people has been recognized as a social problem (Livingstone, 1999). Increasingly, the problem can be characterized as too many credentialed people chasing too few good jobs (Brown, 2006).

An alternative to merely promoting tighter links between school and work recognizes that education and employment systems represent different interests, serve different age groups, have different purposes, are differently organized, are the subject of different policies, and use different policy instruments. Instead of focusing on education as a means of solving economic problems, therefore, more attention should be given to "demand side" issues such as employer investment in training and effective utilization of workers' capabilities in workplaces (Livingstone, 1999, 2009).

2. History matters.
Tracing the development of vocational education and training (VET) in Canada from the beginnings of compulsory schooling in the nineteenth century, Lyons et al. (1991) state, "Canadians have historically considered vocational education to be preparation for second-class citizenship" (p. 137). They add that the system has been hindered by several factors. These include Canada's inheritance of the British system of education (which privileged academic over vocational education); education and training being provincial matters; the country's historical reliance on

immigration to address labour needs; inconsistent VET support from the federal government; and the lack of social partnership between government, industry, and labour around training priorities. These features are important in situating school policies. In addition, it is important to look at changes over time in the labour market and workplace. Situating school reforms within a historical and economic context allows us to appreciate continuities and disjunctures over time while identifying the possibilities and constraints associated with change. We see, for example, that the recent focus on the role of education in developing work skills is not new; this preoccupation recurs in periods of rapid economic change and often stems from employers' concerns. It becomes apparent that policy solutions, in earlier periods and now, tend to focus on enhancing the employability skills of youth.

3. Divergent interests.
A look at the historical development of VET reveals a range of influential players. Consider, for example, the role of employer groups such as the Canadian Manufacturers' Association, which led the campaign for state-supported technical and vocational education in the late 1800s. Their aims were quite different from those of organized labour groups such as the Trades and Labour Congress. More recently, the education reforms promoted by groups such as the Conference Board of Canada can be juxtaposed with the agenda of the Canadian Labour Congress, not to mention classroom teachers. In exploring school policies, then, it is important to be aware of the different interests associated with different visions and the balance of forces pushing education in one direction or another (Taylor, 1997). Differences in interests are partly rooted in tensions within capitalism, since the strategies that employers adopt in order to remain profitable are often inconsistent with popular demands for education (Livingstone, 1994).

Moore and Young (2001) distinguish between two ideologies that have characterized debates over curriculum policy in the UK: *neo-conservative traditionalism* and *technical instrumentalism*. The former tends to see curriculum as a given body of disciplinary knowledge to be transmitted by schools, while the latter places primary importance on economic imperatives and preparing youth for the knowledge-based economy. In other words, while traditionalists see knowledge as an end in itself, technical instrumentalists see it as a means to an end. In Canada, historically, there is evidence of these different views, with industrialists challenging the English grammar school model for compulsory schooling as they campaigned for technical education (Lyons, Randhawa, & Paulson, 1991).

4. What is at stake?

Several agendas are behind debates about educational reform agendas. These include the kind of knowledge that is valued in schools, who controls this knowledge, and who has access to it (cf. Centre for Contemporary Cultural Studies, 1981). In the discussion that follows, I address the persistent problem of the division between academic and vocational curriculum content and delivery. I consider a range of key issues and questions: How did this division develop? Is the valuing of academic over vocational curriculum warranted, and whose interests does it serve? My argument is that educational and labour-market outcomes for students in "academic" course streams tend to be better than in "vocational streams," but this separation of mental and manual activities ultimately fails to serve any students well. The higher status of academic programming in Canadian secondary schools is partly related to the fact that it is well resourced and builds on the existing social and cultural capitals[1] of the mostly middle- and upper-class students who have access to it. If similar resources were allocated to technical and vocational education, status differentials might be reduced.

At the same time, technical instrumentalism has become pervasive in discussion about education in recent years. As Moore and Young (2001) suggest, in the UK context:

> The neo-conservative model is increasingly seen as (a) too slow in the production of knowledge, (b) too inefficient and too elitist to ensure that the majority of the population gain the skills and qualifications they need, and (c) too out of touch with the increasingly competitive global society in which we find ourselves . . . As a result, the universities are under pressure to move away from a reliance on disciplines towards more "connective" transdisciplinary models of knowledge production, and schools are expected to shift from a curriculum based on subjects to one based on modularity, the mixing of academic and vocational studies, and generic skills. (p. 457)

Moore and Young question these shifts, which can also be observed in Canadian education. They argue that while traditionalism takes little account of the changing social context, technical instrumentalism ignores the fact that knowledge has developed within epistemic communities over time. The stark division between theory and practice gives rise to a pendulum swing from traditionalism to instrumentalism; rather than accept this either–or perspective, an alternative would be to allow students and teachers to explore the relationships between theoretical and practical forms of knowledge without diminishing either.

5. Formulating alternatives.

The preceding discussion raises important questions about future directions for secondary school reform. In particular, should schools perpetuate or try to constructively engage the theory–practice divide? Drawing on the work of sociologist Basil Bernstein, Rob Moore (2009) distinguishes between *vertical* and *horizontal* knowledge structures. Vertical structures are "context transcending," and entail the elaboration of meanings so they can be shared across contexts. By contrast, horizontal structures are rooted in local everyday knowledge cultures that are highly context dependent and limited in transferability. "Verticality is achieved through the translation, paraphrasing and integration of terms in a way that allows knowledge to progress to higher levels of generality and abstraction across the contexts of horizontal discourse" (Moore, 2009, p. 57). Both types of knowledge are important, and more work needs to be done in schools to address how connections can be made between them rather than constantly privileging one over the other. In my view, it is crucial that we ask how connectivity can be promoted in the education system. A good example would be to provide opportunities for people to move across knowledge and institutional boundaries.

Theories of learning are relevant to this discussion. In particular, David Guile (2010) draws on the work of Vygotsky to suggest that although everyday and theoretical concepts are formed in different ways, the process by which they are learned is profoundly interconnected. Young (2003) adds that it is the discontinuities between "knowledge" and common sense that enable us to gain knowledge about the world. Thus, a future-oriented curriculum involves providing opportunities for students to cross boundaries between school, the workplace, and everyday life experience. Boundary-crossing involves reconstructing identity, translating activities between the different sites, reflecting on differences between these practices, and collaborating and co-developing new practices—it is not simply a one-directional transfer (Akkerman & Bakker, 2011). Such an approach calls for the development of new types of learning relationships between schools and workplaces, and between teachers, instructors, and students. For example, teachers need to support students in relating their situated knowledge of workplaces to the codified knowledge of the curriculum. The vision of an education-led economy reflected in a connective learning model is more compelling to me than the economy-led education reflected in more traditional models (cf. Young, 1998).

Changing Expectations of Canadian Schools

The claim that educational institutions are failing to produce an adequate supply of skilled workers is not new. Policy-makers, among others, have been arguing this case on and off since the nineteenth century. The underlying assumption is that schools and post-secondary education (PSE) institutions play an important role in producing the human capital needed to contribute to national economic competitiveness (see for example, Canadian Chamber of Commerce, 2014). This role became even more important with the emergence of what has been characterized as a *knowledge economy* in the late twentieth century. Currently, we see human capital theory, which assumes that higher levels of formal education will secure economic productivity, reflected in concerns about high school "drop outs" and the international focus of policy-makers on youth who are "not in education, employment or training" (NEETs). Reports about the increasing percentage of new jobs that require post-secondary education abound (e.g., Miner, 2010). Questions are being raised about whether a high school diploma is sufficient to prepare youth for work in highly skilled workplaces. There are also calls for PSE institutions to provide more work-integrated learning opportunities for students (Canadian Chamber of Commerce, 2014).

Since the early 1990s, there has been a noticeable shift in policy discourse from a singular focus on producing more skilled graduates toward ensuring a better match between their skills and actual labour market requirements. This shift is likely due, at least in part, to the increase in average educational attainment over time. Fifty-three percent of Canadians aged 25 to 64 had some level of tertiary education in 2012—the highest rate among Organisation for Economic Co-operation and Development (OECD) countries (Canadian Education Statistics Council, 2014). However, there are still reports that lament poor adult literacy and numeracy rates (Canadian Chamber of Commerce, 2014). Concerns about job–skills mismatch are also related, no doubt, to concerns about the rise in underemployment among university graduates—to the growing numbers of "baristas with BA's" (Friese, 2012).

The real problem, it has been claimed over and over, is labour-market mismatch: "people without jobs, jobs without people" (Miner, 2010). A CIBC report lists 25 occupations showing signs of skills shortage and 20 with signs of labour surplus (Tal, 2012); a cross-sector survey of Ontario employers reports a range of required credentials, including two- or three-year college diplomas (57 percent), four-year degrees (44 percent), and trades certification (41 percent) (Conference Board, 2013). The now-familiar call for more students to enrol in STEM (science, technology, engineering, and math) subjects is echoed in a 2014 Canadian Chamber of Commerce report. An emergent discourse in education policy advocates for matching youth aspirations with available work, instead of urging more youth to pursue university education.

Groups such as the OECD have also weighed in on debates. Given continuing demand for trades workers and the academic bias of Canadian secondary schools, the OECD (2008) has recommended providing more diverse and vocational curriculum in upper secondary schools, including the development of high school apprenticeship programs. It further recommends providing more workplace-based experiential learning opportunities at both secondary and PSE levels, and providing more intensive programs targeted toward youth who face multiple barriers to employment (e.g., those in remote and rural areas).

In spite of all the debate and the reports, disagreement persists about how educational institutions should respond to labour-market demands, which skills are required, and what level of skills is actually needed. For example, although the Conference Board highlights shortages of skilled labour, other reports suggest that the real problem may be simply that the overall quality of jobs has declined since the late 1980s (Tal, 2013). In addition to the increase in part-time work and self-employment, a key reason for this decline is that job creation in high-paying industries has failed to keep up with the growth in low- and mid-wage industries over this period. Further, although the Conference Board (2013) and Canadian Chamber of Commerce (2014) suggest that employers are most interested in science, engineering, and technology graduates, and in business and financial professionals, a US report suggests that the so-called STEM crisis is more myth than reality given high unemployment rates in related occupations (Anft, 2013).

Since "demand side" assessments produce unclear and contradictory results, educators should take them with a large pinch of salt. The findings of a US study also dispute the Conference Board's (2013) report that "only a handful" of employers surveyed demanded graduates with liberal-arts degrees (p. 24). In fact, more than half of over 300 employers surveyed by the Association of American Colleges and Universities said that recent college graduates should have "both field-specific knowledge and skills and a broad range of skills and knowledge" (Supiano, 2013). Employers and college presidents agreed on the importance of a "twenty-first century liberal-arts education," comprising broad and adaptive learning, personal and social responsibility, and intellectual skills. Thus, age-old disagreement over whether a general (liberal) or practical arts (vocational) education will better prepare youth for the future continues.

This book deals with international themes, which are explored using examples from Canada. I found common threads in vocational education policies since the 1990s in four jurisdictions—Newfoundland and Labrador, Ontario, Alberta, and British Columbia (Taylor, 2007). Policies aimed at helping students transition to work included updating technology curriculum in secondary schools; encouraging partnerships between schools, colleges, and employers to provide training and work-experience opportunities for students; developing youth apprenticeship and dual credit (high school–college) programs where students can earn high school credits while gaining post-secondary training or education; and encouraging more student career planning. Additionally, in Quebec the Ministry of Education highlighted the importance of school–employer partnerships, shared responsibility for training, and diversified pathways for youth (Molgat, Deschenaux, & LeBlanc, 2011). Quebec is somewhat unique in offering CEGEP (Collège d'Enseignement Général et Professionnel) programs after students complete a high school diploma: either a two-year pre-university track or a three-year technical track preparing students for specific occupations. In Nova Scotia, a school–work-transition project was introduced in the mid 1990s to help high school students gain work experience (Thiessen & Looker, 1999). A recent trend has been the increase in school-leaving age from 16 to 18 years, brought in by Ontario, Manitoba, and New Brunswick.[2]

Provincial governments have also set about trying to reform curriculum to better reflect the kind of skills needed by twenty-first-century learners. For example, British Columbia has begun to "overhaul education from kindergarten to post-secondary in pursuit of a new skills-training agenda." This approach claims that students will learn "more usable skills with hands-on, multidisciplinary projects" than they would in the current subject-based approach (Hunter, 2013). Similarly, Alberta's "Inspiring Education" vision for K–12 education shifts the focus of learning from "knowing something" to "knowing how to access information about it," given the authors' conviction that economic competitiveness will rely on "big-picture skills like innovation, creativity and entrepreneurship" (Government of Alberta, 2010, pp. 25, 12). The growing emphasis on inquiry-based learning contradicts the "back-to-basics" and traditional education[3] themes evident in discussions about school reform in the early 1990s (Taylor, 2001). However, the utilitarian focus of those earlier discourses remains.

My overview of provincial policies suggests that there are commonalities and a great deal of policy borrowing across jurisdictions. Therefore, although much of the research presented in this book took place in the provinces of Ontario and Alberta, it is based on programs that are very similar to those in other provinces. For example, most jurisdictions offer high school apprenticeship programs, cooperative education, work experience, and increasingly, dual credit opportunities for students (Taylor, 2007). Enrolments in these programs, however, are uniformly low across the country as a proportion of overall high school enrolments—even in Quebec, with its technical track in CEGEP, only 9 percent of youth aged 15 to 24 held a VET diploma or certificate in 2006 (compared to 4.4 percent for Canada overall) (Molgat et al., 2011). Socio-demographic characteristics of students in VET programs also tend to be similar across sites; for example, a Quebec government report suggested that students in VET programs are usually male, have academic challenges in school, emphasize their manual abilities, and have parents with low levels of schooling and/or who work in jobs requiring little formal training (Molgat et al., 2011).

While there are regional economic differences that need to be acknowledged—for example, the youth unemployment rate in Newfoundland and Labrador was almost double the national rate in 2005 (Taylor, 2007)—my focus on the provinces of Alberta and Ontario captures some of the effects of these differences. Alberta has been an economic powerhouse in Canada largely because of oil sands development, while Ontario has struggled with challenges faced by its much larger manufacturing sector. Alberta's population is also much smaller—just over one-quarter of Ontario's. Therefore, these two provinces provide a good comparison of different vocational education policies and their effects. While I would have liked to include more references to relevant studies in other provinces, unfortunately the literature on the topic of secondary school vocational education is sparse.

Organization of Chapters

Millennial-generation youth are confronting a set of economic circumstances that are quite different from those faced by their baby-boomer parents. Chapter 2 describes why this is the case by exploring some of the economic and policy trends that have impacted work and markets in Canada in the last 50 years. These include globalization and trade liberalization; the shift from a manufacturing to a service economy; an increase in non-standard work forms; a decline in industrial unions; the discourse of a knowledge-based economy; and continued reliance on immigration as a source of skilled labour rather than local investments in training. For youth, the result has been lengthier and more uncertain transitions from education to work. In response, education and training systems have debated what is needed to prepare young people who will be the flexible, adaptable, and highly skilled workers needed in today's "knowledge economy."

Chapter 3 suggests that the expectation that education will contribute to economic prosperity, which has been a focus within secondary and post-secondary educational policy for a few decades, is not new. Historically, this focus has been most evident during periods of rapid economic change and crisis. For example, industrialization in Ontario led to a campaign for technical education and the provincial Technical Education Act of 1897 followed by the federal Industrial Education Act of 1911. Similarly, the growing demand for technical labour was a driver of the Technical and Vocational Training Assistance Act of 1960. Increasing demand for clerical workers similarly led to the expansion of commercial education. In recent years, a utilitarian view of education has again become evident in policy talk. Reasons for this include some of the changes documented in chapter 2, including the rapid changes in work and more globalized competition. However, the examples of curriculum changes in Ontario and Alberta raise questions that persist today: To what extent should vocational education be separated from general education? Is it the purpose of schools to provide students with access to narrow, occupational training? And most importantly, what is the value of different types of work-integrated learning for different groups of students?

Chapter 4 presents findings about youth pathways in Canada based on national data and compares youth transitions in Canada with those in Germany. It also suggests that it is too simple to propose that Canada can merely follow the German example of apprenticeship training, in light of important national differences in school systems, labour-market organization, and institutional structures related to VET. The chapter then discusses policies related to school–work transition in Canada since the early 1990s that attempt to respond to the challenges facing youth, using examples from Ontario and Alberta. I argue that "new vocationalism" is impeded by the legacy of old vocational thinking and structures and neo-liberal education reforms; the latter promote competition among schools and work against attempts to blur academic–vocational divisions in schooling.

Chapter 5 considers questions about the organization of and access to knowledge, which underpin discussions about high school vocational education. This chapter explores the legacy of ideas—beginning with Aristotle and Plato—about the division between theoretical and everyday knowledge, and ensuing debates about the purpose of vocational education in the early 1900s in North America. I then turn to the effects of the academic–vocational division in high schools, and consider how some of these ideas are challenged by interviews with high school apprentices about their learning in schools and workplaces. The chapter concludes with a discussion about approaches to VET that have the potential to challenge the academic–vocational divide.

Chapter 6 considers the effects of course streaming and vocational streaming for different groups of youth. I look at Canadian research into the inequitable outcomes of streaming for students divided by socioeconomic status, race, and gender. Then I present my own research into school choice and school-to-work transitions, focusing on transitions for Indigenous youth in Alberta and the gendered and classed outcomes of high school apprenticeship programs in Ontario and Alberta. At the same time, I discuss ways of disrupting inequitable processes and challenging the devaluation of work-based education.

Finally, chapter 7 concludes with discussion about the shifting aims of vocational education, the implications of reform visions presented in provincial education plans for vocational education, and ideas that could inform policy discussion. My own argument here originates from my analysis of changes in work and in education in recent decades. I argue that a more promising direction would include a "connective" pedagogical approach that does not privilege either codified curricular or situated workplace knowledge. Such an approach could transcend the "either theory or practice" patterns that have bedevilled so much previous educational reform and, as such, would better serve youth facing challenging new economic circumstances.

Chapter 2

"It's the Economy, Stupid!"[1]

I exist in a world in which I don't understand what a 401K[2] is all about.

Social Security will not likely exist by the time I will need it.

I will never have a pension.

I've never even filed for unemployment. Because as a freelancer, I'm never in one place long enough to qualify.

This is not unique to my job description.

This is unique to my generation. (Katherine, 2013—Blog post, US "millennial")[3]

In recent years, much has been made of the challenges associated with intergenerational relations in the workplace. A plethora of books offer advice about how to manage young workers. The issue arises partly because the conditions that shape our understandings of work and learning have changed with breathtaking speed. Older baby boomers may remember workplaces of the 1960s and 1970s without personal computers, where secretaries performed the clerical and communications tasks that many workers now undertake as part of their daily work. Unionized factory work was a viable option for youth leaving school at 16. A man could work his way up the corporate ladder and find success without a degree—although women were still found mainly on the bottom rungs, if at all. A "job for life" was not uncommon. In contrast, "millennials" (or "Generation Y," born in the 1980s) have been raised to expect instability and insecurity. Commentators may note the difficulty of holding the attention and loyalty of Generation Y, but arguably these young workers are simply products of their times as they confront the changing culture of capitalism (Sennett, 2006) as well as shifting occupational opportunities in the global division of labour.

To make sense of the worlds of work and learning faced by contemporary Canadian youth, this chapter documents fundamental, structural changes to labour markets that have occurred over the last half-century. Although this work focuses on Canada, the trends discussed here are global in scope and scale (OECD, 2009). I assume that the way today's youth approach education and career decisions is influenced by changes in the economy and labour markets over time. For example, during recessionary periods, individuals are more likely to pursue further education and training. Although we know that most youth do not engage in simple cost-benefit analyses of their education and job decisions as rational choice theorists suggest, the increasing credential requirements of jobs are likely to influence the educational decisions of young people in an upward direction. In fact, data suggest that most Canadian youth aspire to a university education (Krahn & Taylor, 2005). But at the same time, growing underemployment of well-educated workers and shortages in intermediate skill occupations (e.g., skilled trades) may dampen university aspirations.

This chapter sets the context for later chapters by exploring several economic and policy trends that have impacted work and labour markets in Canada. The trends addressed are:

- Globalizing economy and the liberalization of trade
- Shift from a manufacturing to a service economy
- Increase in non-standard work forms
- Decline in industrial unions
- Policy discourse of a knowledge-based economy and human capital model
- Continuing reliance on immigration as a source of skilled labour, and the reluctance of employers to invest in training

Although these trends are explored individually here, in practice they are deeply interconnected and pose complex policy challenges for youth transitions.

Global Economy and Liberalization of Trade

Canada's culture, political history, and economy have been shaped by its historical development as a settler society and staples economy; in earlier times, exported "staples" included fur, fish, wood, wheat, mined metals, and fossil fuels. Since the signing of the US–Canada Free Trade Agreement (FTA) in 1988, the Canadian government has been an active participant in trade agreements. With the addition of Mexico, the North American Free Trade Agreement (NAFTA) superseded the FTA in 1994. This interest in free trade has intensified; since 2006, Canada has concluded free-trade agreements with at least 38 countries and has begun to deepen trade and investment ties with the largest markets in the world, including the European Union, India, China, and Japan. Recently, Ed Fast, the minister of international trade commented, with reference to the Trans-Pacific Partnership (TPP) trade negotiations:

> Opening new markets around the world to boost Canadian exports and providing the protection to Canadians to invest abroad are key to creating jobs and opportunities for hard-working Canadians in every region of the country. (Government of Canada, October, 2014)

Free-trade agreements are believed to benefit all participating countries because overall productivity gains will be realized when countries direct their resources to their most efficient uses (Kim, 2010). Supporters of free trade argue that "a rising tide lifts all boats" (Sperling, 2007), and that trade liberalization has generated some of its promised efficiencies (Huffbauer & Schott, 2005). However, the impacts of free-trade agreements continue to be debated. Organized labour equates trade liberalization with downward harmonization of labour laws and policies[4] and a more market-oriented economy—in short, a "race to the bottom" for workers. Unions see trade agreements and global economic integration leading to downward pressure because companies aim to compete globally on the basis of lower wages and lower labour standards (Scott, Salas, & Campbell, 2006). For example, a Canadian Labour Congress (CLC) submission to the federal government regarding the Trans-Pacific Partnership negotiations states:

> Over the past 30 years, free trade and investment agreements have increased the downward pressure on wages, contributed to concessionary demands and justified the curtailment of workers' rights, instead of raising standards. (CLC, 2012, pp. 2–3)

The pros and cons of trade liberalization therefore remain contested. Economist Morley Gunderson suggests that the impacts of trade liberalization are not predetermined—harmonization *could* occur in an upward as well as a downward direction, for example, "by such procedures as the emulation of best practices, the uniform application of multinational practices, and concerted political and trade union responses" to trade agreements (1989, p. 22). However, he admits that globalization and trade liberalization increase the pressure to discontinue costly social policies that are more concerned with equity than efficiency.

The implications of economic globalization for the Canadian economy and labour markets include plant shutdowns, job losses through downsizing, corporate reorganization and mergers, and the relocation or expansion of company operations outside Canada (Krahn, Lowe, & Hughes, 2011). Like the US, Canada has experienced deindustrialization as factories have closed or been relocated to areas such as China or India where labour is cheaper, workers have fewer rights, and environmental standards are weaker. As part of this global division of labour, trade liberalization is seen as a "win–win" partnership between "head" nations, which design products, and "body" nations, which manufacture them (Rosecrance, 1999). It is assumed that industrialized countries will become "magnet economies," attracting high skilled–high wage work (Brown & Lauder, 2006).

However, the increased access of transnational corporations (TNCs) to high-skill, low-wage labour presents a serious threat to the North American middle class, as "offshoring" moves up the value chain (Brown, Lauder, & Ashton, 2011). The ability of TNCs to shift aspects of their business to different countries—often in order to take advantage of high-skill, low-wage labour—means that the pressures for downward harmonization of labour policies are currently more intense than those for upward harmonization. As a result, work life is increasingly precarious for many workers.

The Shift from a Manufacturing to a Service Economy

In 1973, Daniel Bell described a coming post-industrial society characterized by the shift from manufacturing to services and the rise of a technical elite. Since then, the decline of the North American manufacturing sector has been well documented. Major recessions in the early 1980s and early 1990s and most recently in 2008 have been felt hardest in this sector, and each recovery has been characterized by a further loss of manufacturing jobs. For example, a writer in *The Atlantic* considers the impact of the 2008 recession:

> When we think about what the [US] economy has lost since the Great Recession [2008 to 2010] we tend to consider it in terms of simple addition and subtraction. We said goodbye to more than eight million jobs in the downturn; we've added around four million back. It's easy and dismal math. But there's another painful dimension to this recovery that's gotten far less attention than the lingering jobs deficit. It's the fact that most of the jobs we

lost offered decent pay, while the ones we're adding are mostly low-level, service sector positions. Middle-class jobs have been replaced by McJobs. (Weissman, 2012)

The diversity of the service sector is reflected in the juxtaposition of "McJobs"—defined as low-paying, low-prestige, dead-end jobs that require few skills and offer very little chance of advancement—with the work of highly skilled "symbolic analysts," as described by Reich (1992) in his book, *The Work of Nations*. Service industries include a wide range of work from retail sales to business services and therefore can be divided into categories based on rewards and status. OECD (2000a) writers define "services" as:

> [A] diverse group of economic activities not directly associated with the manufacture of goods, mining or agriculture. They typically involve the provision of human value added in the form of labour, advice, managerial skill, entertainment, training, intermediation and the like. (p. 6)

While in 2008, over half of employed Canadians worked in *upper-tier services*, 22.6 percent were employed in *lower-tier service jobs*, including higher proportions of women and youth (Krahn, Lowe, & Hughes 2011). Upper-tier services include business, education, health and welfare, and public administration, while lower-tier services include retail trade and other consumer services.

The service sector has expanded significantly across OECD countries in recent decades (OECD 2000a). According to Statistics Canada, 80 percent of all new jobs within Canada between 1992 and 2005 were in the services industry (Canadian Services Coalition & Canadian Chamber of Commerce, 2006). In 2008, 76.5 percent of employed Canadians were employed in services, compared to 47 percent in 1951. The growth in service-sector employment is related to the reduction in the proportion of workers in primary and secondary sectors (extracting or harvesting products and manufacturing finished goods) that occurs as a result of productivity gains. This increased productivity is a consequence of the development of new technologies and production systems, the expanded role of the state as provider of services, and an increasing demand for a wider range of services as individuals' incomes and leisure time increases (Krahn et al., 2011). Between 1987 and 2008 the percentage of workers employed in primary occupations declined from 5.1 percent to 3.2 percent and those in manufacturing declined from 7.7 percent to 5.2 percent (Krahn et al., 2011). In contrast, 12 percent of workers were employed in managerial and professional administrative occupations in 2008, and another 15.1 percent were employed in other administrative and clerical jobs. There has been a pronounced shift from "blue-collar" to "white-collar" work in the past 30 years.

Deindustrialization has been particularly hard on male workers, who have tended to be overrepresented in manufacturing jobs. Writers such as Lois Weis (1990) in the US have written about the implications of de-industrialization of the economy for working-class male youth. She found that the vast majority of male high school students living in the "rustbelt" cities of the Northeastern US in the mid 1980s, like earlier generations of working-class males, continued to expect to earn a family wage, allowing their wives to stay home and look after children despite the disappearance of factory jobs. Most female high school students, on the other hand, aspired to further education and a career, rather than counting on a husband to support them. Changes in identity-formation can thus be related, at least in part, to labour-market changes.

More recent cohorts of youth in Canada are pursuing higher education in large numbers, and young women have surpassed young men as a proportion of undergraduates in universities. A longitudinal study found that a majority of youth in Canada who were initially surveyed at age 18 had pursued post-secondary education by age 24 (Hango & de Broucker, 2007). However, many of these well-educated young adults are spending a number of years in non-standard white-collar jobs before obtaining more secure employment (Krahn et al., 2011). Many find themselves trapped in a student labour market consisting mostly of part-time jobs in lower-tier consumer and retail services. Further, the return on investment in education is less certain, since over the past two decades, post-secondary tuition fees have grown at three times the rate of inflation (Macdonald & Shaker, 2012).

A *Globe and Mail* article entitled "Why Are We Training Our Arts Grads To Be Baristas?" quotes a recent university graduate as saying:

When I finished my MA [Master of Arts] I found myself working at a coffee chain surrounded by fellow students and recent graduates, all of us looking for that "real job" and confused about our fate. (Friese, 2012)

A longitudinal study of earnings found that although initial earnings for social sciences and humanities graduates are lower than for those from more applied fields (e.g., engineering or health), the gap narrows over time (Finnie, Childs, Pavlic & Jevtovic, 2014). But transitions from school to work have, in fact, become extended for most youth—the duration of youth transitions from the end of high school to work increased by nearly two years across 15 OECD countries between 1990 and 1996 (OECD, 2000a). More generally, industrial restructuring and the growth in non-standard work, discussed below, have led to labour-market polarization and rising income inequality in Canada.

The response of students to increased uncertainty varies. While some youth have become more instrumental in their approach to schooling, others appear to be clinging to adolescence and developing priorities that are quite different from their parents. For example, when a high school English teacher in the US polled his class, he found that most students would rather have a "'fun job for their favorite team or band' for $30,000-a-year salary than a 'job that involves analysis and synthesis' for $50,000 a year" (Godsey, 2015).

The Increase in Non-standard Work Forms

The nature of employment is evolving. Evidence from Canada and other OECD countries indicates that the notion of the standard employment relationship based on full time, continuous employment, where the worker has access to good wages and benefits, is no longer the predominant employment structure, to the extent it ever was. In its place, more precarious forms of work have arisen. (Law Commission of Ontario, 2012)

The expectation of "a job for life" was more common in previous generations, although it was by no means universal even then. Today's youth face a very different labour market. Non-standard work forms, including part-time work, contract work, self-employment, and multiple-job holding, have accounted for three of every ten jobs since the late 1980s (Krahn et al., 2011). Some of the shift to non-standard work is related to employers' interest in increasing their flexibility and reducing labour costs in uncertain economic times. In addition, more workers have chosen to become self-employed or to take on a second job.

Overall, non-standard work is characterized by less job security, lower pay, and fewer benefits, and therefore increases the precariousness of employment and income for many workers (Fuller & Vosko, 2008). Unsurprisingly, studies suggest that precarious workers are more likely to report stress and tension at work (Lewchuk, de Wolff, & King, 2007). Non-standard employment may also have long-term earnings costs for workers (Krahn et al., 2011). Since 1997, contract work has surpassed all other forms of temporary employment in the Canadian job market, representing just over half of all temporary jobs in 2009 (Lam, 2010). Contract workers tend to be more educated and slightly younger than permanent workers, and are paid around 14 percent less per hour than their permanent counterparts. They also experience less job security and little or no benefits. In 2008, a little more than one-quarter of 15- to 24-year-old employed Canadians were in a job with a specific end date (Statistics Canada, 2008).

In addition, nearly half of all employed 15- to 24-year-olds in Canada were working part-time between 2000 and 2010 (Krahn et al, 2011). While many of these youth were likely to be students, 16 percent of all part-time workers in 2008 reported working part-time because they could not find full-time work. Youth are also overrepresented in casual employment. A 2009 report indicated that almost half of all casual workers were 25 or younger, and about one-quarter were students (Lam, 2010). The wage gap between seasonal and casual positions and permanent positions was almost 34 percent.

Unpaid work for youth seeking professional experience is also on the rise. In his book *Intern Nation: How to Earn Nothing and Learn Little in the Brave New Economy*, Ross Perlin (2012) documents the trend toward unpaid internships for youth as part of degree requirements or to gain entry to a competitive field. A recent *Globe and Mail* article explores this trend in the Canadian context, noting:

> It's difficult to nail down statistics on interns, as "intern" isn't a title recognized in law. Still, some employment lawyers have taken it on as their cause, citing a growing acceptance of unpaid intern-ships in offices and postsecondary institutions. There's a clear draw for employers, who use internships as a way to save money and nurture talent. (Bascaramurty, 2011)

The decline in economic opportunities for youth has implications for the way that they make education and career decisions. Specifically, some writers have suggested that today's youth are often less loyal to employers and less concerned about following the "normal biog-raphies" of their parents (involving linear movement from school to a full-time work and family formation). This may be because such biog-raphies are less possible in today's "risk society" (Beck, 1992). Just over half of Canadian millennials (those aged 20 to 30 in the job mar-ket) surveyed in 2014 expected to have some experience with contract work (Broadbent Institute, 2014). In addition to extended transitions from education to work, today's youth are living at home with par-ents longer and forming their own families later. They pursue a wider variety of pathways and construct their identities as much through consumption as through production activities (cf. Kenway & Bullen, 2001). The shift toward a more contingent and flexible workforce has led to a more flexible attitude on the part of youth in their definitions of work and career, since job market experience quickly reveals that there are few "careers," most work is short-term, and much of it is unskilled (Dwyer & Wyn, 2001).

The Decline in Unionization

> Two-tier wage deals like those inked recently by Ford Motor Co. and General Motors Co. are spreading across the U.S. border into Canada's labour landscape—again—as companies struggle to compete with lower-cost global rivals. . . . The auto sector is not the only one facing demands for lower wages. Air Canada, which announced last week it will add 900 new jobs in the next year, has also implemented different wage levels, with hires at its new lower-cost discount airline permanently earning less than those at the mainline carrier. (McFarland, 2012)

Economic globalization has given employers an edge in relations between capital and labour. While the unionization rate is much higher in Canada than the US, overall it has decreased gradually over time, falling from 37.2 percent in 1984 to 31.2 percent in 2011 (Krahn et al., 2011; Statistics Canada, 2012). Unionization rates also differ by industry. For example, the strength of unions in manufacturing and other blue-collar occupations has declined because of industrial restructuring, while public sector unionization has grown. Only around one-third of workers in blue-collar occupations were unionized in 2008, while between half and three-quarters of workers in the public sector (e.g., nurses, teachers, professors, and health-care technical and support workers) belonged to a union (Krahn et al., 2011). At the same time, unionization rates in the high-growth areas of retail, finance and insurance, and accommodation and food services, were less than half the national average. Smaller service employers scattered at locations across the country are much more difficult to organize than large industries employing thousands of workers in a single plant (Canadian Press, 2012). Additionally, rates vary between age groups: 36.3 percent of employees aged 45 to 54 belong to a union, compared to 14.3 percent of those aged 15 to 24 (Ore, 2012). Provincial differences are also apparent—in 2011, Quebec had the highest unionization rate at 39.3 percent of Quebec while Alberta had the lowest at 23.2 percent (Statistics Canada, 2012). Unionization rates in Canada tend to be higher in large workplaces and for full-time permanent workers.

The decline in the unionization rates is significant, since a key function of unions is to protect their members from job loss and pay cuts. On average, unionized workers earn about 10 percent more than non-union workers, and are also more likely to have pension plans, more paid vacations and holidays, dental and medical plans, and better job security (Krahn et al., 2011). For youth who, as noted above, are more likely to be employed in non-standard work in the service sector, lack of representation in the workplace may contribute to poorer economic opportunities.

In addition, the question of how youth learn about their rights in the workplace is important. Our research into high school work-experience programs in health care in Alberta indicates that, despite health services being a highly unionized sector, students learned little about unions through these internship programs (Hudson and Taylor, 2011). The declining power of organized labour points to larger questions about the protection of workers in the face of global corporate power. In light of the decreased relevance of unions, these questions have been posed through citizen movements such as "Occupy Wall Street," as well as through discussions about "flexicurity" in Europe—a policy strategy that attempts to combine labour-market flexibility with security for workers.

The Knowledge-Based Economy and Human Capital Discourse

[A] major economic transformation has taken place over the past two decades. This has involved an extension of markets and a retrenchment of government, more open economic borders, a new "technological paradigm" based on microelectronic information and communication technologies, and an ongoing shift to service- and information-based activities. This restructuring, coupled with a range of social, cultural, and demographic changes, has had a significant impact on our working lives. Patterns of workforce participation have changed. Traditional industries, occupations, and communities have declined while new ones have emerged. And the content of work and how it is organized have been evolving rapidly. (Betcherman, McMullen, & Davidman, 1998, p. 1)

Competitiveness in the new economy is seen as tied to human capital, skills, innovation, and technology. According to Beckstead and Vinodrai

(2003), the proportion of the employed knowledge-based labour force increased from almost 14 percent to over 22 percent between 1971 and 1996. Further, by 1996 more than 90 percent of *knowledge workers* (managers and professional and technical workers) had at least some post-secondary education, compared to just over 50 percent in the remainder of the workforce (Beckstead & Vinodrai, 2003). Thus, in the new knowledge-based economy, employment is believed to be moving away from low-skill manual labour toward more complex and rewarding knowledge work. But as noted above, critics point out that the increasing global supply of skilled labour means that the move toward high-skill, low-wage economies is a more likely result.

Implicit in much of this public discourse is the belief that workers are currently not well enough educated for the available work. However, as Livingstone and Scholtz (2007) point out, the reality that "knowledge workers" make up, at most, one-quarter of the labour force means that "three quarters of Canadians still [work] in jobs that involve the routinized transmission of data, the processing of goods, and the delivery of services" (p. 141). These authors argue further that the supply of educated workers is less of a problem than the underutilization of the skills of the current workforce. This underutilization takes a variety of forms, ranging from situations where entry requirements are lower than workers' formal education and skill certification to those where individuals are involuntarily participating in temporary employment. Citing the 2004 *Canadian Learning and Work Survey*, Krahn et al. (2011) confirm that 34 percent of respondents felt underemployed.

As noted in chapter 1, human capital theory stresses the role of formal education in securing economic productivity. It tends to assume that labour-market participants compete for jobs in a single, open labour market, that information about available jobs is widely circulated, that all potential employees with the necessary qualifications have equal access to job openings, and that employers make rational hiring decisions based on an assessment of an individual's ability (Krahn et al., 2011). However, family circumstances, social class background, and geographical location, along with ascribed attributes such as gender, race, and ethnicity have been shown to be equally important determinants of educational and occupational choices and outcomes (Hango & de Broucker, 2007). Certain groups of Canadians are more likely to be underemployed, particularly visible minorities and recent immigrants. This fact challenges the human capital model assumption that a job's rewards are determined by its economic contribution to society (Reitz, 2001). Further, labour-market statistics depicting growing polarization suggest that workplace power is "dynamic, negotiated, struggled over, historical, and lived" (Livingstone & Scholtz, 2007, p. 145).

Policy debates that emphasize the importance of human capital in a knowledge-based economy also raise important questions about the changing demand for skilled labour, the ability of the Canadian education and training system to deliver the skills demanded, and the willingness and ability of employers to provide "good" jobs that utilize graduates' skills. Government policy-makers (Government of Canada, 2002) tend to argue that skill requirements have increased, while critics such as Livingstone (1999) counter that they have, in fact, not increased significantly. Examining the evidence on both sides, economist Michael Smith (2001) agrees that the evidence for an *up-skilling thesis* is not persuasive, but disagrees that the current supply of skills is adequate. Citing the chronic and long-standing shortages in skilled trades, he argues that, while Canada has an adequate general supply of university-educated labour, more attention should be paid to developing intermediate skills—i.e., the technical and cognitive skills not normally associated with university education.

One topic that is often discussed in the media is the perceived shortage of skilled trades. For example, an article in the *Edmonton Journal* suggested that Alberta could be short by as many as 70,000 tradespeople by 2020[5] (Halliday, 2012). In recent decades, provinces across Canada have introduced high school apprenticeship programs in response to such concerns. These programs tend to be promoted as either a debt-free alternative to other forms of post-secondary education for students who prefer "hands-on learning," or a "back-up" plan for university-bound students, given increasingly uncertain returns on post-secondary education (Bartlett, 2012a, 2012b).

Addressing Labour-Market Needs

Canada has historically relied heavily on passive labour-market programs. For example, policy has often favoured immigration over training as a way of increasing the supply of skilled labour (Krahn, 1991). From the recruitment of Chinese rail workers in the 1880s to the current emphasis on the skilled immigrant class in immigration policy, Canada has used immigration as an economic development strategy (Phythian, Walters, & Anisef, 2009). However, the skills mix of recent immigrants arriving in Canada has changed, partly because of the shift in source countries—the proportion of immigrants from countries other than Europe and the US grew from about 5 percent before 1960 to nearly 80 percent in the 1990s (Reitz, 2007). In addition, 69 percent of newcomers aged 25 to 44 years who arrived in Canada between October 2000 and September 2001 had a university education, compared to 22 percent of the Canadian-born population in the same age group (Statistics Canada, 2003). But it is a dismaying fact that many of these highly educated professionals experience the non-recognition of their foreign credentials and devaluation of their foreign work experience (Bauder 2003; Raja, Beaujot, & Woldemicael, 2012).

Perhaps because of growing concerns about immigrants–jobs mismatch, Canada has also begun to rely more on temporary migrant workers in recent years to meet labour needs. The number of workers brought to Canada under the Temporary Foreign Worker Program more than tripled between 2000 and 2011 (reaching 300,111 in 2011) and has exceeded the number of economic class residents entering the country since 2006 (Dauvergne & Marsden, 2014). In consequence, Canadian employers in certain sectors have become dependent upon temporary foreign workers (Foster, 2012). However, migrant workers' limited access to civil, political, and social citizenship rights renders them partial citizens (Taylor & Foster, 2015), and by enforcing "atypical employment relations," migrant worker policies perpetuate inequity between these workers and others (Anderson 2010, p. 313).

Another problem with importing skilled workers is that it tends to reduce the incentive for companies to invest in worker training. In fact, international studies show that Canada has slipped from twelfth to twentieth place in terms of the priority employers place on training their workers (Goldenberg, 2006). For example, fewer than 30 percent of adult workers in Canada participate in job-related education and training, compared to almost 35 percent in the UK and nearly 45 percent in the US. American firms also spend about 50 percent more (as a percentage of their payroll) on training than do Canadian firms. In addition, worker training in Canada is highly concentrated among younger workers, workers with higher education and skill levels, and workers in larger firms (Conference Board of Canada, 2005; Fortin & Parent, 2008; Goldenberg, 2006). Although concerns have been expressed about adult literacy, basic skills training remains at the bottom of training priorities (at only 2.2 percent of total training expenditures) (Goldenberg, 2006, p. 17).

The Canadian vocational education and training (VET) system has also been critiqued for failing to develop the kinds of skills needed in the labour market. It is perceived to be weak compared to countries such as Germany because of the lack of social cooperation and institutionalized links between schools, colleges, and employers (Schuetze, 2003). Further, in Canada in-school vocational programs continue to be stigmatized, since they were historically developed for "at risk" students and "low academic achievers" (Schuetze, 2003, p. 71). Statistics also reflect systemic differences: while Germany's dual system of vocational education and training involves about two-thirds of each school-leaving cohort, Canada's high school apprenticeship programs involve only a small fraction of that (Heinz & Taylor, 2005). Meanwhile, Canada and the US have the dubious distinction among OECD countries of having the highest proportion of young adults with post-secondary education diplomas or degrees working in low-skill jobs (Saunders, 2008).

These findings, along with the academic focus of the education system, support the argument of Smith (2001) and others (Schuetze & Sweet, 2003) that Canada has done a comparatively poor job of developing intermediate skills. A much higher proportion of youth aspire to attend a university rather than college or technical institute (Krahn & Taylor, 2005). However, a university education is no guarantee that graduates will find work related to their field of study. For example, the *Globe and Mail* ran a series of articles in 2012 about the need to "transform the ivory tower" of higher education in order to promote the kinds of skills needed by leaders in the global economy.

An article in that series described 28-year old Paul, who was working at a Toronto gym as a receptionist while taking additional online university courses to help him secure a teaching job (Andersen, 2012). Despite his undergraduate and graduate degrees in education and history, Paul had been unable to even find work supply teaching. He was in debt and was wondering about the value of his university education given that his job at the gym required only high school education. The author sees the cause of such problems as the failure of higher education to change with the times, and specifically, to prepare graduates who have the kind of skills demanded by employers—problem solving, written skills, social intelligence and adaptive thinking.

However, the experiences of today's youth suggest that policy-makers should focus on how occupational opportunities are being transformed in the global division of labour, not just on the supply of marketable skills (Brown, Lauder, & Ashton, 2011). As noted in chapter 1, policy discourse has shifted over time from a focus on increasing overall skill levels to better matching skills to areas of labour market demand.

The Implications of Economic Changes for Youth Transitions

> For Canadian youth, it is essential [that] the education or training they get is relevant to the job market they will enter. First, they need to know where the jobs will be. Second, they need to know what those jobs will be so they can plan their education and training accordingly. Third, they need education that is not just job training but equips them to be adaptable. (CEO and President, Canadian Chamber of Commerce, 2014)

In his classic 1977 book, *Learning to Labour*, Paul Willis writes of the resistance of British working-class "lads" to an education system that they saw as irrelevant to their futures as workers on "the shop floor." Ten years later, Phillip Brown's book, *Schooling Ordinary Kids* (1987) presented a different picture, partly reflecting a change in economic conditions. While, for the "lads" in the 1970s many unskilled manual jobs were still available, this was less the case by the 1980s. In response to this changed situation, the majority of working-class youth aimed to complete their schooling with the hopes of securing better jobs. But Brown cautioned that rising youth unemployment could present a crisis for secondary schools, as too many youth chase too few good jobs.

A key message from the preceding discussion of changes in work and in labour markets is that today's youth are confronting a set of circumstances that are very different from those faced by their parents. A recent survey of freshmen in the US found that many see their undergraduate education as the first step in a long journey, and more than half already plan to do a Master's degree (Berrett & Hoover, 2015). However, youth are often given advice that may lead to tensions: aim high *but* don't have unrealistic expectations; follow your passion *but* enrol in programs that clearly lead to a job; work hard and be loyal to your employer *but* be prepared for several career changes in your lifetime. No wonder many of these individuals are confused and emotionally distressed.[6]

In contemporary Canadian society, economic changes continue to affect youth, making their transitions longer and more complex (OECD, 2000b). Today's youth spend more time in formal education and delay their entry into the adult labour market. An analysis of a longitudinal survey of youth in Canada acknowledges that the normative path of finishing school, starting a full-time job, marrying, and then starting a family has become far less common in recent decades (Hango & de Broucker, 2007). Similarly, a longitudinal study of over 1,000 Alberta high school students who graduated in 1996 found that by 2003 a large minority had deviated from a high school to university pathway, either returning to upgrade, transferring programs, transferring institutions, or dropping out of a post-secondary program (Krahn & Hudson, 2006). Evidence thus suggests that transition processes have become more uncertain, fragmented, and individualized.

Writers also admit that the idea of a linear pathway was only ever applicable to a minority of young people, and therefore researchers need to explore both the conditions under which different groups of young people are living and the meanings that they attach to life events (Dwyer & Wyn, 2001). For example, Looker and Dwyer's (1998) findings from longitudinal studies of youth in Canada and Australia suggest that the transition experiences of rural youth are quite different from those of urban youth, because of the extent to which educational decisions are intertwined with decisions about work, marriage, parenting, and geographical mobility. As a result, rural youth are less likely to follow a "linear pathway." Studies also reveal that Aboriginal youth are likely to leave the education system with much lower levels of educational attainment than non-Aboriginal youth, frequently returning later to upgrade (Hango & de Broucker, 2007).

In sum, youth transitions to employment in Canada reflect historical, social, and regional differences as well as sweeping labour-market changes. A common response to education–jobs mismatch from ministries of education across Canada has been the introduction of school-to-work transition (SWT) initiatives to help develop young people's "employability skills" and clarify their career pathways (Lackey, 2004; Taylor & Lehmann, 2002), discussed in chapter 4. But educational and training policies that assume the need to simply increase skill levels are limited, given the existence of pockets of skills shortage amid underemployment and unemployment. With other writers (Brown et al., 2011; Krahn et al. 2011; Livingstone, 1999), I argue that attention to the "supply" of skills must be complemented by greater focus on the utilization of skills in the workplace and training as well as on initiatives that increase worker voice and control. In addition, discussions about the role of education systems in preparing workers need to be more attentive to changes in work over time and the challenges facing young graduates.

Chapter 3

Education for Industrial Purposes

Jeannie Oakes and Martin Lipton (2007) suggest that different purposes for American education have been emphasized in different historical periods. For example, in the period of nation-building in the 1830s, the role of the common school in teaching citizenship skills was prioritized. More than a century later, with the launch of Sputnik by the Soviets in the late 1950s and the Cold War, the role of schooling in ensuring national security was emphasized. This was followed by an emphasis on schools solving social problems stemming from poverty, racism, inequality, urban decay, and cultural unrest in the 1960s and 1970s. Oakes and Lipton note that since the 1980s and the publication of *A Nation at Risk*, the US has focused on the role of schooling in boosting the nation's economic competitiveness. Arguably, the discourse of the role of schools in securing individual and national economic prosperity continues into the present. Thus, school reforms tend to reflect social trends of the day.

But school reforms also reflect struggles over different visions for education. For example, Wirth (1974) suggests that the vocational education movement in the US between 1900 and the passage of the Smith-Hughes Act in 1917 involved important debates over how young people should be prepared for their work roles. On one side, "social efficiency" proponents such as David Snedden and Charles Prosser believed that the task of education was to make the economy function more efficiently, that social inequality was inevitable, and that children should be fitted for their place in society. They were impressed by the dual system of education and training in Germany, and argued that vocational education in the US should also constitute a separate system of education that would train students for employment by instilling habits of correct thinking and doing; such an education would operate like a workplace.

On the other side, John Dewey advocated for a vocational education that would alter the existing industrial system rather than adapt workers to it (Drost, 1977). He was opposed to the separation of trade education and general education because he thought that it would make both kinds of training narrower and less significant. Instead, Dewey proposed an approach that would reorganize traditional education to utilize the subject matter of the everyday environment. His aim was to combine democratic and humanistic values with science and industry. This debate is discussed further in chapter 5, which looks more closely at the academic–vocational divide.

Debates about whether schools should organize curriculum into academic or vocational streams and direct students into distinct programs continue to be relevant. This chapter looks more carefully at the recurring emphasis on the economic purposes of education during periods of rapid economic change and crisis (Taylor, 1997). It also examines struggles within and across stakeholder groups (e.g., business, organized labour, educators) that partly reflect class-based interests. I focus on the campaign for vocational education and the rise of commercial education in the late 1800s in Canada before turning to examples of school reforms in Ontario and Alberta since the 1960s. While, as the previous chapter indicates, changes in the economy and labour markets require new ideas about how to best prepare youth, a historical perspective helps us see patterns and understand the significance of changes.

First, it is useful to clarify what is meant by *vocational education*. It was defined by the Canadian Teachers' Federation in 1987 as education that is directed toward the teaching of skills and knowledge that are useful in occupations for which post-secondary education is not required, and which may help graduating students qualify for entry-level positions in these occupations (cited in Smaller, 2003). A broader definition is provided by British writers, who suggest that the term *vocational* refers to educational functions and processes that prepare and equip individuals and groups for working life (Skillbeck, Connell, Lowe, & Tait, 1994). This broader definition is more appropriate given the current belief that youth need more than a high school diploma to be successful in the labour market.

To describe vocationally oriented curricula, provincial education systems have also shifted from language such as *industrial* and *practical arts* toward terms such as *technology education* (e.g., Career and Technology

Studies in Alberta; Technological Education in Ontario). The scope of vocational curriculum has also broadened to include a wide range of occupational areas; for example, technological education curriculum in Ontario includes communications technology, computer technology, construction technology, green industries, hairstyling and aesthetics, hospitality and tourism, manufacturing, technological design, and transportation technology.[1] The discussion that follows focuses on changes in vocational–education related secondary school policies since the late 1800s.

The Establishment of Industrial Education[2]

The period from approximately 1868 until 1911 involved various efforts to establish industrial education programs in Ontario schools. At that time, the Canadian economy was predominantly agricultural, but manufacturing was becoming important, contributing 19 percent to the gross national product by 1870 (Palmer, 1983). By 1871, 57 percent of the workforce in Toronto was employed in factory-like settings with greater than 50 employees. However, the 1870s were also marked by a major depression that took its toll on workers and small producers. The 1880s saw increasing consolidation of competitive capital in Canada, characterized by an emergent monopoly capitalist economy and complex new technology and production processes (Heron, 1986). Enlargement of the scale and outputs of manufacturing gave rise to the view that more skilled labour was required to sustain economic growth in Ontario (Morrison, 1974).

The beginning of manual training and technical education in Ontario was said to involve attempts to combat and control pauperism and crime among urban children (Bullen, 1989). According to Morrison (1974), a small group of prominent Torontonians proposed creating a set of industrial schools in 1868 to provide vagrant children with the moral habits thought to be lacking in their homes. Out of this meeting, an Industrial Schools Committee formed, which petitioned municipal authorities and then the provincial government with a plan to provide special schools. This led to an amendment of the 1871 School Act, which empowered school boards to establish industrial schools.

Private initiatives paved the way for subsequent government legislation (Semple, 1964). For example, the Industrial Schools Association of Toronto established a school where boys would learn the work norms and rules of the factory in 1887. In 1891, a small group of municipal, educational, and industrial leaders established the Toronto Technical School, with municipal funding (Stamp, 1972). A board with representatives from the Canadian Manufacturers' Association and the Toronto

Trades and Labour Council administered this school. In 1900, the MacDonald Manual Training Plan, established by a tobacco millionaire, established 21 manual training schools across the country (Smaller, 2003). Such schools provided business groups with examples of the workability of school-based manual training (Morrison, 1974). During this period, local boards of trade became involved in the campaign for technical education at provincial and national levels. An article in the *Mail and Empire* in 1899 argued for technical education to increase Canada's competitiveness and provide a better fit between schools and the workplace (Stamp, 1972).

These activities provided the impetus for Ontario's Technical Education Act of 1897, which allowed school trustees to establish technical schools or add technical schools to existing high schools, making it possible for schools such as the Toronto Technical School to become part of the Board of Education. However, without additional resources provided for these schools, little change occurred (Stamp, 1972). By 1900, the Canadian Manufacturers' Association (CMA) had taken the reins in the campaign for technical education (Lyons, Randhawa, & Paulson, 1991). For example, in a 1901 address, the president of the CMA pointed to the progress made by countries such as Germany, the UK, and the United States in technical education, and indicated the need for Canada to move in this direction. Significantly, in the provincial election of 1905, support for industrial education was an important part of the Conservatives' winning platform. During the election campaign, the CMA was active in voicing concerns about the shortage of skilled labour and the education of youth who were not destined for university and professional work (Stamp, 1972).

On the other hand, the Trades and Labour Congress, as the voice of labour, was skeptical of claims about a labour shortage and felt that technical education might produce a surplus of qualified workers. While the group eventually lent support to "technical education" (founded on the theoretical principles underlying a trade), it objected to "manual training" (specific trade training), in part because it was thought to limit social mobility for children from working-class families (Bullen, 1989; Morrison, 1974). In the debates of this time, educators tended to be divided between technical education supporters and "traditionalists" who eschewed close connections between practical economic life and schooling (Stamp, 1972). This recalls Moore and Young's (2001) reference to long-standing ideological debates between neo-conservative traditionalists and technical instrumentalists in the UK, noted in chapter 1.

In 1909, Superintendent of Education John Seath was charged with the task of examining technical education in the United States and

Europe and making recommendations for the Ontario system (Stamp, 1972). His priorities were improving the quality of teaching, tailoring the curriculum to the vocational needs of students, and keeping children in school longer (Lloyd, 1985). Part of Seath's work involved visiting schools in America, England, Scotland, France, Germany, and Switzerland. His report, *Education for Industrial Purposes* (1910) proposed a framework for vocational education in Ontario that included differentiated schools, governance of technical schools by a school board–industry–labour advisory committee, and a teachers' college for training industrial teachers. The recommended separation between vocational and general education was more in line with the vision of Snedden and Prosser described above than with the more integrative approach of Dewey.

Also in 1910, federal labour minister Mackenzie King (later prime minister from 1921 to 1948) was appointed to lead a Royal Commission on Industrial Training and Technical Education. The Royal Commission was Canada's first federal commission on education and was concerned with all aspects of vocational education at all levels (although there was some confusion over whether jurisdiction for vocational education lay with the federal government or the provinces) (Lyons et al., 1991). The Commission report recommended massive federal funding for the broad field of vocational education.

Meanwhile, in Ontario, the Industrial Education Act of 1911, based on Seath's recommendations, provided a framework for technical education and a generous and systematic formula of provincial grants. Stamp (1972) concludes, "it was the combined work of educators, industrialists and governments that produced the comprehensive system of technical education ultimately adopted in the province of Ontario" (p. 73).

At the same time, as noted above, business, organized labour, and different groups of educators tended to respond in different ways to questions such as:

- What role should schools play in preparing youth for work?
- Is technical education likely to increase or decrease equity in schools?
- Should schools be training youth for specific jobs or developing more general academic skills?
- Should schools provide a comprehensive education or educate youth in different streams?

Such questions have continued to be relevant since the 1911 Act.

Complementing activities in Ontario, the federal government introduced the Agriculture Aid Act of 1912, which allocated funding for the support of agricultural education for one year (Lyons et al.,

1991).[3] The Technical Education Act of 1919 (following the Royal Commission) provided additional funding to underwrite the expansion of provincial training systems and infrastructure. Under its terms, the federal government was to provide $10 million to the provinces over 10 years to promote technical education at the secondary school level. Although funding regulations restricted participation of poorer provinces, between 1918 and 1939 the number of technical and industrial day schools in Ontario increased from 11 to 62 (Lyons et al., 1991; Manzer, 1994). Further, the linking of vocational education and training with industrial policy was evident at that time and in the decades that followed (Fisher et al., 2006).

There are a few key messages to be taken from the preceding discussion. First, business groups were important players in the development of vocational education between 1870 and 1940, in terms of both lobbying governments and developing models. Second, governments and industry groups were concerned about the nation's competitiveness and were interested in the applicability of international models to the Canadian context. Third, although some writers suggest that a consensus was reached among different players in the development of vocational education, ideological differences were evident. For example, labour groups were more concerned that the role of education as an equalizer of opportunity be maintained and strengthened, while employers wished to ensure a supply of labour by tightening links between schools and the workplace. In an interesting parallel with today, educators in the late 1800s were debating questions around whether schools should be focusing more attention on youth who were going directly to work (at that time, around 95 percent of the school population) rather than those entering universities and professional vocations (Stamp, 1972). Thus, vocational education was a site of struggle between different interests.

The Expansion of Commercial Education

An examination of the expansion of commercial education, which occurred in the last half of the nineteenth century, reveals competing interests and demonstrates the gendered and classed nature of vocationalism (Jackson & Gaskell, 1987). In the early years of commercial education, the majority of students were middle-class males, and classes focused on penmanship, bookkeeping, and business law (Jackson & Gaskell, 1987). Around this time, grammar schools prepared students for a range of occupations. In the mid 1860s, Egerton Ryerson began a campaign to separate classical from more practical education; the 1871 School Act differentiated *collegiate* institutes (reserved for the classical education of boys) from *high schools* (where boys and girls received instruction in English and "commercial education"). However, in practice, both collegiates and high schools offered educational programs that prepared boys and girls for a range of occupations as well as for university entrance (Jackson & Gaskell, 1987).

Toward the end of the nineteenth century, there was significant growth and reorganization of clerical work; jobs became more specialized and hierarchically ordered, and lower-level jobs were feminized. In 1911, "women represented 53 percent of junior clerical positions and only 12 percent of general clerks" (Jackson & Gaskell, 1987, p. 184); they earned lower wages than men, but better wages than other women workers. The growing demand for clerical workers was accompanied by a growth in private business colleges and a proliferation of commercial education courses. In 1885, a commercial diploma course was introduced in Ontario secondary schools, and in 1911, John Seath recommended dividing the commercial program into a four-year general business course for entry into more managerial positions and a three-year office course, which was further subdivided into accountancy and shorthand (Jackson & Gaskell, 1987).

High school program offerings were distributed between schools—for example, Toronto Central High School provided clerical and other technical training programs, while Harbord Collegiate Institute, a few blocks away, offered only academic programming (Marks, 1986). Data from Toronto's Central High School of Commerce from 1911 to 1930 suggest that males were overrepresented in general business and accounting courses and females were overrepresented in stenography and secretarial courses. Commercial education was well established in the schools of Ontario and British Columbia by the time of the Technical Education Act in 1919. While commercial education had mostly enrolled middle-class students in its early decades, with the introduction of streaming in the 1920s and 1930s, it became more oriented toward working-class students (Jackson & Gaskell, 1987).

In sum, Jackson and Gaskell's (1987) analysis of the development of commercial education from 1870 to 1920 suggests that influences included the growth of clerical work, responses by public school business educators to the growth of private colleges, and popular support for practically oriented education. In terms of forces and players, the development of commercial education differed from the campaign for technical education. Crucially, Jackson and Gaskell highlight the role of vocational schooling in producing gender differences and inequalities.

The Technical and Vocational Training Assistance Act of 1960[4]

The depression of the 1930s limited the development of vocational education in most parts of Canada because of fiscal constraints in the public sector (Lyons et al., 1991). But in 1942, the federal government responded to increased demand for training by passing the Vocational Training Coordination Act, which promised federal funding for a variety of programs for "servicemen, veterans, the unemployed, and supervisors in industry" (Lyons et al., 1991, p. 142). The Vocational Schools Assistance Agreement (1945) also provided federal, shared-cost assistance to create provincial composite high schools. Still, the 1957 Royal Commission on Canada's Economic Prospects noted that the country was not expanding its skilled workforce to meet the need for higher-level skills in an increasingly technological and professional society (Bryce, 1970). The Commission predicted that requirements for a skilled workforce were likely to outpace supply, that immigration could no longer be relied upon as the major source for skilled workers, and that the most severe shortages would involve professional workers. It was believed that the "baby boomers" would be a good source of skilled and professional workers if adequate training facilities could be made available. Apprenticeship training and programs in technical and vocational schools were seen as a way of providing young people with the skills necessary to find employment in a technologically advanced society.

In 1960, the federal Technical and Vocational Training Assistance Act (TVTAA) was introduced to address demands for a more highly skilled workforce, with a focus on both youth and adults. TVTAA was a significant direct intervention, not only in post-secondary education but also in secondary education, which went beyond the federal government's constitutional mandate (Fisher et al., 2006). Bell (2004) suggests that the Act was introduced partly to counter resistance to vocational education in Canada, to address the need for new schools due to the postwar baby boom, and to respond to economic stagnation and rising unemployment in the late 1950s. The assumption was that human capital investment would spur industrial growth.

The main groups served by the TVTAA were non-college-bound youth in schools and individuals who could benefit from training for trade or technical occupations (Young, 1992). The Act addressed programs ranging from high school vocational education to vocational teacher training to apprenticeship training. Over the Act's six-year life (1960 to 1966), the government directed $1.5 billion into capital and operating costs for provincial technical and vocational institutions, including vocational training facilities at secondary schools (Bell, 2004). The funds provided under the Act functioned as a major impetus for the establishment of provincial community college systems in Canada (Dennison & Gallagher, 1986).

The federal government also funded the building of new secondary schools, requiring that half of the space in these schools be devoted to technical and vocational training subjects. Ottawa agreed to share costs of high school programs with the provinces and to reimburse them for part of their expenditures for construction, purchase, or alteration of facilities; salaries for instructors; and equipment costs (Young, 1992). The Act created 662 new schools over six years, and ended partly because of federal–provincial differences regarding the spending of funds. Alberta, for example, spent most of its federal funding on expanding existing composite high schools and building new ones, while the federal government was more interested in developing specific vocational and technical education programs outside of the school system (Bryce, 1970). With TVTAA funding, *composite education* (i.e., separate educational tracks for different groups of students within the same school) became the hegemonic form of secondary education in most provinces (Manzer, 1994).

The TVTAA reflected dominant ideas of the time and, consequently, was supported by the Economic Council of Canada (ECC), which had been established in 1963 as a national advisory body to provide economic and social policy research and education (Smith, 1997). The ECC was a strong advocate of human capital theory and the economic importance of education (Fisher et al., 2006). In its 1965 *Annual Report*, it argued that the creation and maintenance of "an adequate supply of professional, technical, managerial and other highly skilled manpower" was vital for future growth in the Canadian economy (Fisher et al., 2006, p. 32).

But in 1966, the federal government abruptly withdrew from vocational education; federal officials felt that the provinces were neglecting educational programs that were not cost-shared with Ottawa: "At a federal–provincial conference in October 1966, the federal government announced it would withdraw from the field of vocational education to enter that of adult occupational training and retraining, and to increase its assistance to universities" (Lyons et al., 1991, p. 143). The federal government began to take responsibility for short-term training, leaving long-term vocational preparation to the provinces. It also began to focus more on gathering information and brokering partnerships with provinces, employers, and the education system with respect to school-to-work transitions (Marquardt, 1998). This withdrawal was challenging for provinces and school boards that had become dependent on federal funding for high school vocational programs. But despite its abrupt cessation, the TVTAA left a legacy, evident in the following discussion about policies in Ontario and Alberta after the Act.

Ontario since the TVTAA

With the passage of the TVTAA in 1960, the composition of Ontario schools changed in a short time. Education Minister John Robarts reformed the secondary school curriculum to permit the streaming of students into technical/vocational programs, resulting in the construction of 335 new schools and additions to 83 existing schools, all dedicated to technical and vocational education (Smaller, 2003). Between 1961 and 1966, the percentage of high school students enrolled in non-academic programs almost doubled—increasing from 24 to 46 percent of the total school population—while the number of students in academic programs dropped. The 1962 Robarts Plan divided Ontario secondary school curriculum into arts and science; business and commerce; and science, technology and trades. Each branch was offered as a five-year program leading to university and as a four-year program leading to newly created community colleges. In addition, a Diversified Occupations Program was designed to address the needs of students aged 15 or older who were likely to leave school at age 16 by providing them with a Certificate of Training, and special schools were built to deliver this program (Freeman, 2007).

Certain groups of students were more likely to be found in such technical and vocational programs—it is not coincidental that most vocational schools in Toronto were built in working-class/immigrant neighbourhoods (Smaller, 2003). Further, students in non-university course streams were less likely to graduate from high school, according to an Ontario Ministry of Education study (Karp, 1988). Thus, one concern with program streaming arose from the poorer outcomes associated with vocational programs (Smaller, 2003). By the end of the 1960s, vocational education programs were perceived as "dumping grounds" for lower-achieving students in preparation for insecure, low-paying jobs (Lazerson & Dunn, 1977, p. 291). In response to this perception, the 1968 Hall-Dennis Report advocated a fully comprehensive public education, with the idea that training for specific trades or occupations would be left to post-secondary institutions (Manzer, 1994). Comprehensive schools attempted to provide broad opportunities for academic, general, and vocational education for all students without differentiating them by program. A credit system was introduced with individual timetables and promotion by subject, and in some cases, the removal of provincial exams. Thus, comprehensive education became the dominant ideal of policy-makers in the late 1960s and early 1970s.

But the pendulum swung back again when a crisis in the world capitalist economy in the 1970s reignited fears in Canada and other industrialized countries about their ability to compete in the global economy. Neo-liberal policy approaches promoting a less interventionist state became popular in several industrialized countries, including Canada. At the same time, business organizations began to take a renewed interest in the role of education in preparing young people for work. A back-to-basics movement developed during the 1970s and 1980s, and the principles and practices of comprehensive secondary education were attacked. Provincial governments began to revert back to models of the 1950s and 1960s that included increasing requirements for high school graduation, reinstituting a system of provincial exams, and streaming students (Gaskell, 1992). However, students resisted such streaming—Smaller (2003) notes that the number of technology courses taken by Ontario secondary school students in 1996 was only 257,000 compared to 481,000 in 1973, despite an increase of over 100,000 in the student population.

The *Radwanski Report* (1987) in Ontario reinforced the idea that education was the main determinant of collective and individual economic well-being. Reports by the Ontario Premier's Council (*People and Skills in the New Global Economy*, 1990) and the ECC (*A Lot to Learn*, 1992) fuelled the discourse of education for economic prosperity, which was rooted in human capital ideas (Taylor, 2001). These reports promoted the importance of education in the acquisition of basic knowledge and skills, the need for external evaluation of system outcomes (e.g., through expanded provincial testing), and an expansion of the policy community beyond traditional education groups (Manzer, 1994).

But opinions were divided about when students should be streamed into diversified programs. While the *Radwanski Report* recommended that secondary schools offer a common curriculum, the ECC and Premier's Council reports proposed that they offer more diversified academic and vocational courses (Manzer, 1994). The emphasis on more diversified programs in secondary schools was reinforced in the 1995 *Report of the Royal Commission on Learning* (RCL), which recommended de-streaming from grades 1 to 9 and specialization in grades 10 to 12. Other RCL recommendations included providing two sets of courses—one designed for university preparation and the other, of equal quality, designed to emphasize applications and connections outside of the classroom (Gidney, 1999).

The New Democratic government followed the recommendation to de-stream grade 9 soon after being elected in 1990, but this decision was reversed by the Conservatives. Beginning in 1996, the newly elected Conservatives introduced a series of legislative acts and cabinet decisions that changed curriculum, funding, and the governance of schools. Curriculum changes included new high school course streams: students in grades 9 and 10 could take academic or applied courses, while grade 11 and 12 students could take workplace, college, university/college (U/C), or university "destination" courses. Curricula were developed in consultation with universities, colleges, and businesses to ensure that courses would better prepare students for post-secondary education and the world of work (Kitigawa, 1998). Another aim was to increase graduation rates. While the number of compulsory credits was increased, with more focus on math, languages, and science, technology courses continued to be optional.

Reforms in Ontario between 1960 and the mid 1990s reflect the view of education as a tool of industrial development. During this period, there was continual struggle over the content, organization, and delivery of curriculum. Today, questions about the pros and cons of streaming students persist; schools are both shaped by and shape existing patterns of social inequality and stratification through their processes of sorting, rewarding, and certifying graduates (Davies & Guppy, 2014). Chapter 6 looks more closely at the processes and outcomes of streaming for different groups of students.

Alberta since the TVTAA

Arguably, debates about streaming in Alberta have been more muted than in Ontario since the 1960s, although there have been similar discussions about how to organize secondary school programs for students. The *Worth Report* (Commission on Educational Planning, 1972), commissioned by the Social Credit government in Alberta and released by the newly elected Conservative government, and the *Harder Report*, released five years later, reveal very different perspectives (Curriculum Policies Board, 1977). Mazurek (1999) argues that, while the *Worth Report* reflected the 1960s shift toward student-centred inquiry learning, curricular options, and open classrooms, the *Harder Report* was consistent with a "back-to-basics" approach with less program flexibility.

Both reports acknowledged the importance of vocational education, albeit in different ways. The *Worth Report* spoke generally about the need for more effective planning of schooling to meet occupational needs and the need to integrate occupational placements into secondary schools

(Ritter, 1978). The *Harder Report* was more prescriptive, listing the need to develop the knowledge, skills, attitudes, and habits required of the world of work as one of six objectives of education (Curriculum Policies Board, 1977). It recommended that a minimum number of junior and senior high school credits in the practical arts—industrial education, home economics, business education, or work experience—be required. These credits would be awarded on the basis of demonstrated competencies as well as attendance. The *Harder Report* further recommended developing more courses locally and paying more attention to industry requirements in certain occupational areas. In fact, an appendix to the report listed industry requirements as well as high school offerings and enrolments in 1975–6 (Curriculum Policies Board, pp. 47–54).

In the 1980s and 1990s, the department of education in Alberta continued to focus on making educational programs more relevant to changing political, social, and economic realities. The 1984 *Review of Secondary Programs*, commissioned by Education Minister Dave King, stated that secondary education should "provide the initial stages of career preparation by developing basic work skills, with an emphasis on fostering appropriate attitudes and awareness of the world of work" in addition to other goals (Alberta Education, 1984, volume 1, p. 5). The review carried forward a number of issues and recommendations made in the 1977 *Harder Report*; for example, it mandated courses in practical arts and business.

In the late 1980s, the Integrated Occupational Program (IOP) was introduced—a separate program for students aged 12.5 to 19 years who were at risk of not graduating from high school. The IOP, like the Diversified Occupations Program in Ontario, was a separate path, leading to a Certificate of Achievement for students who completed 80 credits—20 credits less than the minimum required for a high school diploma (Alberta Education, 1998). Of these 80 credits, at least 27 credits were to be in academic courses, 13 in optional courses, and 40 in IOP courses. IOP curriculum was designed to provide concrete learning experiences, and occupational courses were to include off-campus learning, job shadowing, and mentoring. However, as with vocational programs in Ontario, concerns emerged that the program was inflexible and outcomes for students were poor.

The 1984 review laid the groundwork for the 1988 *Practical Arts Review*, undertaken by the Curriculum Design Branch. Toward the end of the 1980s, the Ministry of Education decided that the practical arts curriculum must be updated to "help students prepare to enter the workforce . . . with the skills, knowledge and attitudes needed to help to ensure Alberta a competitive place within the global trading community"

(Curriculum Development Branch, 1989, p. 4). The *Practical Arts Review* focused on courses in junior and senior high school home economics, business education, industrial education, personal development, and work-experience education. The assumption undergirding this focus was that the old practical arts curriculum did not adequately prepare students for knowledge-economy work. In addition to economic changes, the review was prompted by concerns about declining enrolments in practical arts subjects, aging of equipment, and underutilization of facilities. Studies by Alberta Education and by the Calgary and Edmonton public school boards indicated reduced student enrolment in most practical arts courses since the mid 1980s (Curriculum Development Branch, 1989, p. 20). As noted, a similar enrolment decline was occurring nationally and internationally (Smaller, 2003).

The *Practical Arts Review* aimed to revitalize curriculum and promote equity of access by updating old courses and developing new courses to reflect changes in society and in the world of work (Curriculum Development Branch, 1989, p. 16). Technology was also to be integrated into all practical arts courses, as reflected by the new name: Career and Technology Studies (CTS). Gradwell (1999) suggests that emphasizing technology skills was a strategy adopted by provinces across Canada to increase the status of practical arts courses. A *new vocationalism* discourse was emerging (Lehmann & Taylor, 2003).

A Vision for the Nineties (Alberta Education, 1991), *Meeting the Challenge: Three-Year Business Plan* (Alberta Education, 1994), and the *Framework for Enhancing Business Involvement in Education* (Alberta Education, 1996) continued to highlight the importance of work education to economic prosperity in Alberta. The "vision" document stated that the new CTS curriculum would provide students with "a combination of academic and practical skills as preparation for future study and careers in highly skilled and technical fields" (Alberta Education, 1991 p. 10). The three-year business plan for education specifically mentioned that business would be "a key player in defining the specific learning requirements of industry" (Alberta Education, 1994, p. 6). Schools would be accountable for students' achievement of provincial learning standards, "including employability skills consistent with workplace requirements" (p. 5); success or lack thereof would be gauged via satisfaction surveys of employers, post-secondary instructors, parents, and students. The *Framework for Enhancing Business Involvement* was part of the implementation of the business plan and recommended creating a Career Education Foundation to promote business–education partnerships; promoting workplace learning and apprenticeships; enhancing the image of trade, service, and technical careers; reviewing school programs and standards to ensure greater attention to employability and entrepreneurship; reviewing diploma requirements to decide whether a certain number of CTS credits should be required; and involving business/employers more in policy-making at all levels. The policy focus on flexibility and partnership with the business community was not unique to Alberta, but could also be observed in other Canadian jurisdictions (see Gaskell & Rubenson [2004] for a discussion of vocational education reform in British Columbia).

Policies in Alberta, as in Ontario, reflect tensions between the desire to improve linkages between school and work for youth and concerns about streaming students prematurely, thereby closing off other options. For example, partly in response to concerns that the program was inflexible and outcomes were poor, a government report, *Removing Barriers to High School Completion* (Alberta Learning, 2001), recommended that IOP students complete a high school diploma (rather than a certificate) and that the curriculum be redesigned. Although there was less discussion about the overrepresentation of certain groups of students in IOP (e.g., Aboriginal youth), the stigmatization of such vocational programs was recognized. Again, questions arise regarding the roles of schools in shaping patterns of inequality.

As noted in chapter 1, educational policy trends across Canadian provinces since the early 1990s have been quite similar. Concerns about the effect of global economic restructuring on Canadian youth have resulted in policies focused on keeping youth in school longer, encouraging career planning, providing off-campus work-experience opportunities, and making smoother transitions to work.

The examples of Ontario and Alberta suggest that the utilitarian focus on schooling for work has continued since the TVTAA. However, there are growing concerns about a lack of coordination of vocational and training programs across provinces. In response, a national education and training strategy has been suggested as a way to address skills mismatch and high unemployment rates by more closely linking secondary and post-secondary educational curricula to market demand (Ovsey, 2013).

"The More Things Change, the More They Stay the Same?"

This chapter's discussion of the historical development of vocational education suggests continuities and changes over time. Today, as in the past, there is a focus on education as an industrial tool. Some stakeholder perspectives and dynamics have been consistent. For example, business groups have remained interested in promoting instrumental views about education, and the extent to which governments have privileged their interests in policy echoes earlier periods. There continues to be a strong tendency for education reform discourse to be economistic—i.e., concerned primarily with up-skilling the workforce to gain a competitive advantage in the global marketplace. Now, as in the late 1870s, vocational initiatives continue to be "technicist," with the primary focus on providing students with the skills and competencies desired by employers (see Hager and Hyland's 2003 critique of similar trends in England and Wales).

But there have also been significant changes since the late 1800s in work, working conditions, and expectations about work. Chapter 2 argued that fundamental, structural changes to labour markets have occurred over the last half-century, including a shift from a manufacturing to a service economy, employer demands for higher levels of certification, and more non-standard work. More youth today are experiencing non-linear, extended transitions from school to the labour market. But, in comparison with past eras, a much higher proportion of youth today graduate from Canadian secondary schools. Also, in addition to literacy and numeracy, digital technology literacy has become a priority for schools and students.

As more youth attend college and university in a race for credentials, Davies and Guppy (2014) posit that educational selection has moved upwards, with post-secondary education becoming more stratified and high schools less so. Certainly a higher proportion of students graduate from Canadian secondary schools today than did in the past. Shavit and Blossfield's (1993) cross-national research confirms that educational systems tend to open up "step-by-step from the bottom up," although they also note that educational selection continues to favour children of privileged social origins (p. 14). I agree that post-secondary education has become more stratified but argue in chapter 6 that high school streaming continues to contribute to inequitable outcomes.

The above examples of curriculum changes in Ontario and Alberta since the TVTAA support the idea that secondary schools have become less overtly selective over time. In the 1960s, when a much smaller proportion of students attended college and university, vocational streaming by program in composite schools was common. Separate pathways were designed for youth who were seen as destined for work. But by the 1990s, streaming by course within comprehensive schools had become the norm. This change reflects the recognition that a high school diploma has become a minimum requirement for participation in the "knowledge economy." It also reflects increasing demand for access to post-secondary education on the part of youth. Most youth beginning high school today aspire to achieve at least one university degree (Krahn & Taylor, 2005).

However, there are reasons to question whether changes in education are sufficient to ensure "parity of esteem" for areas of schooling seen as vocational. For example, Freeman's (2007) longitudinal study of "ABC" technical school in Ontario suggests that educational practices and technical school resources have not kept pace with labour-market changes. She writes:

> Despite the policy intent in 1990 and again in 2000 to reorganize technical subjects into broad-based technological studies [in Ontario], ABC's shops have continued as old world high-touch rather than high-tech. (p. 10)

Since the end of the TVTAA, provincial governments have adopted a "market" approach to vocational education in secondary schools, which relies heavily on developing private-sector partnerships to deliver programs out of school rather than investing in school-based vocational education programs. This approach perpetuates the separation of programs such as high school apprenticeship and work-experience courses from general education, is likely to reinforce "narrow task-based occupationalism," and arguably represents an "ethically vacuous approach" to vocational studies (Hager & Hyland, 2003, pp. 14, 22). Borrowing from Dewey, Hager and Hyland suggest, in contrast, that VET programs should be underpinned by the social, moral, and aesthetic values that are an integral part of all working lives. Chapter 4 will look more closely at whether these criticisms are justified in relation to new vocational approaches in secondary schooling.

Chapter 4

NEETS, PINES, and "New Vocationalism"

From 2008 to 2010, the proportion of young people not in employment, education or training in the youth population, the *"NEET"* rate, increased by 2.1 percentage points to reach 15.8 percent as an average of OECD countries. (International Labor Organization (ILO), 2013)[1]

The Organisation for Economic Co-operation and Development (OECD) defines PINEs as "young people [who] often have qualifications (diplomas or degrees); they frequently go back and forth between temporary jobs, unemployment and/or inactivity, even during periods of strong economic growth" (Bell & Benes, 2012, p. vi).

Chapter 2 discussed changes in work in recent decades that have significantly impacted youth and other labour-market entrants. Following chapter 3's discussion of the history of vocational education in Canada, this chapter looks in more detail at policy discourses around school-to-work transitions since the early 1990s. Canadian discussions occur within a global context in which concerns are commonly expressed about outcomes for youth, particularly NEETs (youth not in employment, education, or training) and PINEs (poorly integrated new entrants).[2]

Concerns about skills mismatch and PINEs in advanced economies are related partly to the labour-market challenges facing low-skilled youth; as noted in chapter 2, many of these youth work in low-paying, dead-end "McJobs" (Coupland, 1991). But in contrast to historical concerns about the need to produce a greater number of skilled workers through VET, there is evidence that today's young people (aged 15–29) experience both more undereducation *and* more underemployment than workers aged 30 and above. Solutions to these problems have been discussed in a variety of national and international forums. For example, strategies to improve youth employment in G20 countries identified by an Employment Task Force included strengthening quality apprenticeship systems and other school-to-work transition programs in collaboration with social partners; providing career guidance and facilitating acquisition of work experience; and supporting youth entrepreneurship measures (OECD & ILO, 2011). Most OECD countries have moved in the direction of vocationalization of basic and post-compulsory school curricula since the early 1970s, while less industrialized countries have been concerned with enlarging and updating the vocational dimension of the education systems that they inherited from the colonial past (Skillbeck, Connell, Lowe, & Tait, 1994).

Although there appears to be consistency in policy directions globally, differences in national VET systems and national policy approaches play an important role in how individual countries respond to perceived gaps between educational provision and social and economic needs. National differences in labour-market organization, wage-setting mechanisms, work organization, and other institutional structures across different countries are documented in comparative research (e.g., Crouch & Streeck, 2006). Writers have grouped different countries into *liberal*, *social market*, and *social democratic* regimes on the basis of distinct policy approaches (e.g., Green & Janmaat, 2011). Canada, alongside the UK and the US, represents the liberal model; Northwestern European countries such as Germany, Austria, Switzerland, and Belgium represent the social market model; and the Nordic countries represent the social democratic model. Similarly, writers have referred to different varieties of capitalism; for example, *liberal-market economies* in North America and *coordinated market economies* in continental Europe tend to pursue different policies (Hall & Soskice, 2001).

In terms of education, Gleeson and Keep (2004) add that nations with strong traditions of social democracy and well-developed notions of citizenship—the Nordic countries, for instance—may be more likely to maintain wider, societal goals for education (such as education for citizenship) than nations where notions of citizenship have more limited political and cultural resonance (e.g., the UK). Walther (2006) adds to the discussion by examining different transition regimes that include *universalistic* (e.g., Sweden), *liberal* (e.g., UK), and *employment-focused* (e.g., Germany). The universalistic regime assumes individuals' motivation for personal development; youth is therefore seen as a phase of development rather than a resource for society (Stolz & Gonon, 2012). In contrast, a liberal regime aims to prepare individuals for economic independence and tends to individualize the risks of exclusion. Unlike in the universalistic model, government does not regulate vocational education. Since the employment-focused transition regime works to allocate youth to occupational careers and social position, low-achieving students are at risk of exclusion.

National differences in intellectual and political traditions and their institutional manifestations mean that comparisons of outcomes data should be approached with care. For example, Canadian policy-makers often speak with envy about the German apprenticeship system, neglecting to discuss how that system developed, how it has been supported institutionally, and how it is different from the liberal-market approach to VET adopted in Canada. Of course, there are also differences across Canada; provincial jurisdiction over education makes it difficult to talk about a national education and training strategy, which many commentators see as problematic (e.g., Ovsey, 2013). As noted in chapter 3, since the TVTAA in the 1960s, the federal government in Canada has played a less direct role in this area.

This chapter considers what we know about youth pathways in Canada, based on national data, and then compares the Canadian VET system with the German VET system. I then examine policy discourses around school-to-work transitions in Canada since the early 1990s, including discourses promoted by business and governments around school–business partnerships as well as the new vocationalism and K–14 pathways.[3] Last, I discuss specific provincial initiatives in Ontario and Alberta including high school apprenticeship, cooperative education programs, and dual credit initiatives.

Youth Pathways in Canada

In 2005, Canadian Policy Research Networks, a non-partisan socio-economic think tank, launched a project called Pathways for Youth to the Labour Market, which included studies of youth pathways, school policies, career development, and case studies of interesting initiatives. The reports produced provide a useful overview of school-to-work transitions for youth in Canada (Bell & Bezanson, 2006; Doray, Ménard, & Adouane, 2008; Hango & de Broucker, 2007; Krahn & Hudson, 2006; McCrea Silva, & Phillips, 2007; Saunders, 2008; Taylor, 2007).

Using data from the longitudinal Youth in Transition Survey of Canadian youth aged 18 to 20, Hango and de Broucker (2007) identified 10 paths these youth followed between 2000 and 2004. Paths depict youth as "high school droppers," "second chancers" (youth who returned to complete high school), "PSE non-completers," and so on. An earlier study using the same dataset found that by age 20, 85 percent of respondents had graduated from high school (Bowlby & McMullen,

2002). Of those attending PSE, almost one-third attended university; more than half attended community college, university/college, or CEGEP (in Quebec); seven percent attended a trade or technical school; and five percent, a private business or training school. Similarly, a longitudinal study of 1996 high school graduates in Alberta (Krahn & Hudson, 2006) found that 88 percent had enrolled in a PSE program and 60 percent had acquired at least one PSE credential by 2003—32 percent had a university degree, 15 percent had a college diploma, 15 percent had a technical school diploma, and four percent had an apprenticeship certification. A key finding of all three studies is that non-linear pathways were common: for example, returning to secondary school for upgrading, taking a "gap" year, transferring PSE institutions, and dropping out of programs.

Findings confirm that the rate of PSE participation is higher in Canada than in other OECD countries. However, the rate of "overqualification" (or underuse of education) is also more common (Saunders, 2008). De Broucker (2005) notes that one-third of employed 25- to 29-year-olds with a PSE diploma or degree in Canada and the US had low-skill jobs, the highest proportion among OECD countries. In addition, the proportion of workers under 25 years of age who felt overqualified for their jobs was highest in Canada (24 percent) compared to 16 other OECD countries (Brisbois, 2003). The Alberta study found that an even higher rate of employed youth around 25 years of age (31 percent) felt overqualified for their jobs (Krahn & Hudson, 2006). Accordingly, education–jobs mismatch is perceived to be a serious problem. In particular, there is growing concern about the capacity of the Canadian labour market to provide rewarding careers for all who attain PSE credentials (Brisbois, Orton, & Saunders, 2008). Perhaps for this reason, there is increasing interest in high school apprenticeship programs and other school-to-work initiatives directed at producing intermediate skills.

Comparing Canada and Germany

As noted, it is problematic to compare education and training policies across countries without acknowledging differences in institutional structures, including the duration of and extent of streaming in primary and secondary education, access to and duration of PSE, and differences in state regulation of linkages between the education system, labour market, and careers (Heinz & Taylor, 2005). A comparison of Canada and Germany highlights some of these differences.

One significant difference is that, unlike Germany, Canada lacks a tradition of social partnership (Heinz, 2003). Canadian employers have tended to under-invest in workplace learning, and governments have traditionally played a less active role in labour-market policy. Further, the labour market in Canada is different from that in Germany, in that job requirements are often firm specific, and educational credentials and occupations are not clearly linked (Lehmann, 2007). In contrast, Germany's labour market involves a wide range of federally regulated occupations with clearly defined training.

In addition to differences in labour markets, there is also variation in education systems. As noted in chapter 3, comprehensive schools are consistent with the North American goal of providing large numbers of students with a general education and the possibility of pursuing PSE. The current structure of Canadian education includes an elementary education of between five and eight years, followed by secondary education that ends at grade 12. The college system provides vocational and technical programs in specific areas as well as general education. In the province of Quebec, secondary education ends after grade 11 and students go to general and vocational colleges (CEGEPs) where they follow a two-year pre-university program or a three-year technical program. As noted, a high proportion of Canadian youth pursue PSE compared to other OECD countries—as in the US, a "college for all" mentality is pervasive (Rosenbaum, 2001).

In contrast, the German apprenticeship system relies strongly on a streamed general education system (Lehmann, 2007). Streaming occurs at the end of grade 4 (around age 10 or 11) when aptitude tests and parental decisions determine whether a student is placed into lower, middle, or higher secondary schools (Heinz & Taylor, 2005). The lower stream has traditionally led to apprenticeships in crafts and skilled trades, the middle stream grooms students for apprenticeships in commerce, services, and technology, and the higher stream prepares a small group for university entrance. In the 1990s, the vast majority of each youth cohort attained a vocational certificate and a total of approximately 80 percent attained either a vocational certificate or a higher education degree (Heinz & Taylor, 2005).

As in Canada, the main transition routes from school to work in Germany include apprenticeship, college and private training, and university education. However, in Canada less than 10 percent of youth pursue high school apprenticeships, whereas in Germany high school apprenticeship is the main route, travelled by about two-thirds of each school-leaving cohort (Heinz & Taylor, 2005). In the mid 1990s, the German apprenticeship system included 370 occupations—more than double Canada's 150 "apprenticeable" trades (Schuetze, 2003; Tremblay & LeBot, 2003). The German dual system of apprenticeship training consists of a combination of on-the-job training and school-based vocational education over three or four years and is regulated by the German Vocational Training and Education Act, which defines the rights and responsibilities of employers, unions, and government. A federal VET agency develops, reforms, and evaluates guidelines for craft, technical, commercial, and service occupations.

In Germany, the VET system tends to be viewed as a collective good, benefitting employers, youth, and civic society. Vocational training in companies is valued because firms are more likely to have up-to-date equipment, and company trainers are more able to integrate new technical demands into training (Lehmann, 2000). Further, training directives developed for in-company training define vocational school curricula. Employers determine the company's needs and offer training contracts, but workers are also represented in all institutions and committees dealing with VET (Lehmann, 2000). The federal government oversees training in firms and defines the duration of training, job description, knowledge and capabilities, and achievement criteria. Training is also regulated by employer organizations that assess whether trainers qualify to offer vocational training, provide information to companies, supervise the quality of apprentices' training, and certify trainees. The legislative framework brings vocational schools and firms together in a training partnership that results in a lower proportion of unskilled workers among school-leavers compared to North America (Heinz & Taylor, 2005). It is also significant that industry-wide bargaining leads to minimal wage differentials between companies, and therefore there is less poaching of workers. Accordingly, employers are more willing to invest in training.

Comparing the two countries, Lehmann (2000) concludes that the Canadian system provides more *flexibility* for youth to change direction but less *transparency* of pathways, whereas the opposite is true in the German system. While there is less concern about education–jobs mismatch in Germany, early school tracking is likely to restrict young people's access to occupations and training opportunities (Heinz, 2000). In particular, the lower-level *Hauptschule* has become known in many urban areas as the school for the children of foreign workers, immigrants, and economically marginalized groups (Lehmann, 2007). Further, while the German system opens more vocational education opportunities for youth who do not aspire to university, it may not be sufficiently responsive to the changes in skill demands associated with a "knowledge economy."

To a degree, global economic changes are causing policy convergence across countries, with German decision-makers aiming to make education and training pathways more flexible and Canadians looking to render pathways more transparent. For example, in the late 1990s the Ministry of Education in Ontario began to require school boards to provide school–work-transition programs for students intending to enter the workforce after high school (Government of Ontario, 2003). This is part of an attempt to address the academic bias of schools and the purported shortage of intermediate skills.

"New Vocationalism" and Educational Policies in Canadian Provinces

The force behind the growing emphasis on vocationalism in education policy in the UK, according to Hayward (2004), has been the increasing involvement of the business community in education systems, both at the level of policy and in terms of the funding and practices of colleges and schools. Similarly, in Canada we can trace the growing interest in vocationalism to increasing employer interest in school–business partnerships. In the early 1990s, the Conference Board of Canada, an organization representing mostly large corporate employers, began to hold annual conferences on business–education collaboration (Taylor, 2001). In 1990, it established a National Business and Education Centre to help its members develop strategies to work with the education system (particularly at the high school level) to ensure that Canada's youth would be prepared to meet workplace needs. It was thought that stronger links between schools and businesses were needed to address problems such as high illiteracy and dropout rates, areas of weak student performance on international achievement tests, and a lack of science and technology graduates. This attitude was echoed by governments: in 1992, the Economic Council of Canada produced a report called *A Lot to Learn*, which recommended strengthening links between school and the world of work as well as increasing the quality of education by introducing competition, choice, and greater educational accountability.

At the same time, the question of how to prepare youth for a knowledge economy ignited a discourse of *new vocationalism* in North America (Lehmann & Taylor, 2003). New vocationalism has been described as a more "progressive" approach to vocational education, conceived of as broader, better integrated with academic content, and more critical of workplace practices and systems of employment (Grubb, 1996; Sedunary, 1996). Responding to the criticism that "American vocationalism was too narrowly focused on specific utilitarian and practical skills and capacities that quickly become obsolete" (Bills, 2009, p. 132), new vocationalism advocates for providing more inclusive general workforce preparation that integrates academic and vocational learning (Benson

1997; Young 1998). The idea is to make academic knowledge more meaningful and accessible to the majority of students, while using young people's interest in work as a vehicle through which they can critically explore the economic and social structures of society (cf. Avis, 2004).

Some British writers use the term *new vocationalism* in a slightly different way, referring more generally to the resurgence of interest in the vocational role of education and training internationally since the early 1970s (Skillbeck, Connell, Lowe, & Tait, 1994). These authors provide useful definitions of *education*, *vocational*, and *training*:

> "Education" [is] a comprehensive term for purposive, structured human and social formation, governed by intellectual and ethical principles, directed at knowledge, understanding and their applications and informed by a spirit of critical inquiry. "Vocational" refers to those educational functions and processes which purport to prepare and equip individuals and groups for working life whether or not in the form of paid employment. "Training" is task specific but nevertheless, in our usage, a part of education and subject to the values, criteria and principles which govern educational processes generally, even though, as frequently used, its reference is to factual knowledge and unreflective skills. (p. 3)

Similar to writers such as Norton Grubb in the US, Skillbeck et al. (1994) highlight John Dewey's view of vocationalism as involving a "philosophy of purposive activity designed to accomplish results and render service," while also noting the more functional side of vocationalism as servicing the economy (p. 5). Thus, new vocationalism appeals to advocates of social justice as well as proponents of economic efficiency (cf. Hickox 1995). Lorna Unwin (2004), also writing out of the UK, argues for a more expanded view of vocational education; she asserts that it should be seen as involving integrated, holistic practices that make no distinction between knowledge (knowing) and skill (doing). This model of vocational education is about "practical relevance"—both "specific capabilities and principles of procedure, concepts, ideas and skills that are generalisable, capable of application in varied and changing circumstances, and able to be built upon, developed and extended through acquired knowledge, experience, and further systematic studies" (Skillbeck et al., p. 18). The implication is that new vocationalism needs to move away from the dualisms of theory/practice, mind/body, head/hand that characterize old vocational approaches. This theme is echoed in recommendations for the unification of post-compulsory education and training systems (Raffe et al., 1998).

Turning to examples of reforms in the provinces of Ontario and Alberta, I argue that increased emphasis on competition and choice, and reliance on voluntary VET partnerships make it difficult to realize the ideals of new vocationalism.

Ontario

> The Fraser Institute released its report card on Ontario secondary schools a year or so ago and I looked very closely at the criteria they use to judge how successful a school is and one of them was the percentage of advanced courses taken at the school. So the school will in fact be punished for offering workplace destination courses. (High school apprenticeship coordinator, cited in Taylor & Spevak, 2003, p. 23)

In the late 1990s, the Conservative provincial government under Premier Mike Harris introduced new high school course streams linked to workplace, college, and university destinations. While the intent of this reform was to make pathways for students more transparent, an evaluation of outcomes found that failure rates were high in applied courses, and the graduation rate of the first cohort of the new secondary school program after four years was significantly lower than the five-year graduation rate of the previous system (King, 2004). To graduate with a high school diploma, students were required to complete 30 credits (18 required), 40 hours of community volunteer work, and pass a literacy test or course equivalent (Taylor, 2007). Technology credits made up around 9 percent of all secondary school credits earned in 2004–5. The province also required all school districts to provide school-to-work transition (SWT) programs for students intending to enter the workplace after high school.

Following the direction provided by the Conference Board of Canada, provincial governments looked to business to play a greater role in schooling. In 1999, the Provincial Partnership Council became a volunteer advisory committee of the Government of Ontario, comprising leaders from the private, public, and voluntary sectors. Its mandate was to ensure that every Ontario high school student had the opportunity to participate in relevant experiences that would support their academic achievement, career development, and future success.[4] The same year, the Ontario Business Education Partnership (OBEP) was established as a not-for-profit organization that would advocate on key issues impacting youth career exploration and workforce development.[5] As one of its first initiatives, the OBEP coordinated a campaign, "Passport to Prosperity," that encouraged employers to engage with schools. OBEP members primarily include representatives from business/educational councils and industry/education councils, organizations established with provincial support in the mid 1980s to help broker relationships between school districts and local employers (Taylor, 2005).

Elected in 2003, the McGuinty Liberals continued the direction of trying to forge tighter links between schools and post-secondary institutions and employers. In the early 2000s, the Ministry of Education and Ministry of Training, Colleges, and Universities (MTCU) began to fund vocational programs, including the Ontario Youth Apprenticeship Program, School–College Work Initiative, and Specialist High Skills Major program (Taylor, 2009).

The Ontario Youth Apprenticeship Program (OYAP) allows high school students who are at least 16 years of age to gain on-the-job experience in a skilled trade while earning cooperative education credits toward the completion of their high school diploma. Students work with school coordinators to find a sponsoring employer and are eligible to register as apprentices. A small proportion take an accelerated program like OYAP, where they complete the first level of in-class technical training while in high school, but the majority of these students participate in on-the-job training only. Fewer than 5 percent of high school students participate in OYAP, and participation is approximately two and a half times higher for males than for females (King et al., 2005).

The aim of the School–College Work Initiative (SCWI) is to build province-wide articulation between secondary schools and community colleges in order to clarify pathways for youth and encourage more students to select college as their first choice for post-secondary study. SCWI activities include aligning curricula between secondary schools and colleges (Taylor, 2007). Developing seamless transitions between secondary and post-secondary education for a wider range of students is consistent with the high-skills, knowledge-economy vision for education and training. As in programs in the US (Hoffman et al., 2007), a goal and priority for SCWI has been to expand participation in *dual credit* projects—many related to apprenticeship training—to all colleges and boards. Dual credit courses involve a college credit course team-taught by a secondary school teacher, a college teacher, or a certified journeyperson. SCWI reflects the growing interest in K–14 education in Canada and the US as a way to increase high school graduation rates, post-secondary education preparedness, and college retention and graduation rates. This model is reflected in US President Barack Obama's recent proposal to provide students with two years of free community college tuition (Simon, 2015).

The Specialist High Skills Major program (SHSM) initiative, modeled loosely on "Career Academies" in the US,[6] was part of a $1.3 billion multi-year Student Success Strategy introduced by the government to improve high school graduation rates (Ministry of Education, 2003). SHSM allows students to orient their high school program toward different industry sectors by "bundling" courses in their area of interest to match post-secondary, apprenticeship, or workplace learning requirements. The program is intended to have broad appeal for students who plan to go to work, college, or university (Taylor, 2007). The Student Success Strategy also includes legislation that requires students to keep learning in a classroom, apprenticeship, or workplace training program until age 18 or graduation (Bill 52). SHSM involves schools partnering with local communities, sector councils, unions, and employer associations.

OYAP, SCWI, and SHSM collectively reflect an interest in valuing and promoting non-university pathways to students. However, my research into high school apprenticeship programs reveals tensions within SWT programs in Ontario (Taylor, 2005, 2010). In particular, there are contradictions between ideas of new vocationalism and the continuation of an academic/vocational divide, between the focus on the creativity and knowledge-producing potential of the workforce and the presumption that work-based learning is primarily aimed at preparing disaffected young people for the disciplines of the workplace (cf. Avis, 2004).

The Government of Ontario's "Pathways to Success" document (2003) expresses a traditional vocational view that SWT programs should target "at risk" students—those having difficulty meeting diploma requirements, who are disengaged, and who seem destined to go directly to work after secondary school. Similarly, a high school technology teacher who was involved in coordinating an OYAP in carpentry notes the existence of old vocational views about who should pursue apprenticeship training:

> There is reluctance in some schools to feel that their students should transfer to another school and be part of an OYAP program. Because quite often it's not the student they'd like to see go. Quite often, it's the ones they consider some of the brighter students. They think it's a shame that they're throwing their life away. (Taylor, 2006a, p. 325)

The idea that apprenticeship is for "less able" students is pervasive. However, the comments of a representative from a building trades union challenge this out-dated view:

Years ago, when you were not too sharp academically, you became a tradesperson or a janitor or a garbage man, but because of the change in the industry and the technology in the industry there's not as many openings like that for the low end. You've got to learn on a regular basis, for the rest of your life, so you need to be able to have the basic skills to learn and grow, and be prepared for what the next change is in technology that's gonna change our industry to one extent or the other. (Taylor, 2010, p. 509)

From this perspective, apprenticeship must be seen as a high-quality training route because it requires exposure to applied theoretical knowledge in the classroom as an important precursor to on-the-job training (Clarke & Winch, 2004; Keep & Payne, 2002). Yet, a persistent view of apprenticeship and dual credit programs as targeting youth "at risk" reflects the legacy of old vocational thinking. Further, the small proportion of students enrolling in technology courses reflects the reality that school curriculum is, by and large, unaffected by the requirement that schools provide SWT programs.

Tensions over the target demographic of vocational programs also reflect the divergent interests of the partners involved, including the two ministries that coordinate high school apprenticeship and colleges: while the education ministry is focused on increasing high school completion rates, MTCU is more concerned about success for post-secondary students and maintaining the integrity of credentials. This goal diversity is apparent in discussions about OYAP. For example, a representative from MTCU argues that students "at risk" are *not* the target group for OYAP:

Typically there's still a connection made between "at risk" kids and kids that don't learn in an academic setting. . . . Johnny can't do math so we'll send Johnny down to the auto shop. Well Johnny's going to have a tough time doing auto as well if he can't do math. So I think slowly that message is getting through. . . . Kids and their parents and guidance counsellors, etcetera aren't all that well aware of the rigors of apprenticeship training. (Taylor, 2010, p. 510)

Similarly, college administrators were focused on maintaining standards. For example, a college staff person comments:

The key issue that we struggled with is, you know, who is the "dual credit learner," because we're being told [by the provincial government that] we want the "at risk" and the "disengaged learner." Well yes, you can be "at risk" and it may not be an academic issue but you can also be "at risk" because of your academics. And we certainly don't want to muddy our own marketing waters by saying, you know, if you can't succeed in high school come on down to college, you know it's that easy. . . .Wow, we have a problem on our hands if we think we can lower the bar to come to college. (Taylor, 2010, p. 511)

This discussion suggests that Ontario secondary school reforms aim to help ease youth transitions to further education and the labour market by developing school–college and school–business partnerships. Reforms are driven by the idea that education needs to be re-tooled to help students make appropriate career decisions while addressing employer needs for an educated, skilled labour force. However, in reality, programs such as youth apprenticeship continue to be constructed as programs for youth "at risk" rather than for those who may have other post-secondary options. Further, the education of students who aspire to university (over half of first-year high school students) has changed little. As I discuss further in chapter 6, university-bound students tend to be disproportionately from families with high-earning, high-education parents. Therefore, education paths are perceived to differ in terms of the advantage they provide in the competition for jobs, income, social standing, and prestige (Marginson, 1997).

Alberta

So many of our kids default into the workplace, no clue what they want to do. . . we find them back in our post-secondary system, but by now they're 27 years old. . . . So what does that do to the productivity of the country? . . . the bottom line is how do you come down to an orderly transition between education and the workplace? (Interview with Alberta Member of Legislative Assembly [MLA], cited in Taylor, 2002)

Education reforms in the early 1990s under Premier Ralph Klein's Conservative government in Alberta were driven by fiscal constraint and an interest in school choice, testing, and accountability. Ideas about reinventing government to operate more like the private sector in terms of efficiency and accountability were popular at the time (Osborne & Gaebler, 1993). In 1994, the provincial government released its first three-year business plan for education. Under this plan, Alberta became the only province in Canada to introduce charter school legislation;

other reforms focused on centralizing school funding, expanding pro-vincial testing, and mandating school councils (Taylor, 2001).

Implementation teams were established to operationalize the business plan. These included a team charged with "improving business involve-ment and technology integration," which later split into two groups: one concerned with business involvement and another with technology integration. The former developed a working group with business rep-resentatives, educators, and government (organized labour did not par-ticipate) and produced a *Framework for Enhancing Business Involvement in Education* that was released by the education department in May 1996. Recommendations included developing a provincial Career Education Foundation, promoting the image of trades, service, and technical ca-reers through high school programs, and increasing the involvement of business in policy-making, at all levels (Taylor, 2002). The career foun-dation came to fruition in 1997 as CAREERS: The Next Generation, which developed out of a 1994 pilot project that was initiated by the Alberta Chamber of Resources and the provincial government and was intended to address youth employability and the pending skills shortage in the trades.

There are similarities between the kind of SWT initiatives undertaken in Ontario and Alberta since 1990. For example, both provinces oper-ate high school apprenticeship programs and both governments provide financial support to organizations that play a school–business partner-ship brokering role. However, in the Alberta context employers have arguably been more influential—in particular, large energy-sector com-panies. Business concerns about labour shortages and the advocacy of groups such as the Alberta Chamber of Resources were key drivers in the development of the Registered Apprenticeship Program (RAP) in the early 1990s. (Students can apply to RAP in their first year of high school and are then registered as apprentices; once in the program, they earn credits toward their high school diploma through on-the-job training.)

CAREERS: The Next Generation, mentioned above, is similarly in-dustry driven. It is a not-for-profit foundation that aims to link work-place and classroom learning, promote pathways to careers, and develop a skilled workforce for industry in Alberta. Significantly, the majority of its board of directors comes from business and government. CAREERS employs field directors who are responsible for delivering programs in areas of high labour-market demand (e.g., trades, industrial technolo-gies, and health services). Therefore, while it plays a similar role to OBEP in Ontario, CAREERS reflects the regional labour market.

In a program similar to the School–College Work Initiative, Alberta also experimented in the 1990s with the idea of "Tech Prep," based on

US models. Tech Prep programs (later called Career Prep) were first introduced in central Alberta in 1995, before being adopted in different parts of the province. The goal of such programs was to help students explore career choices, set career goals, and work toward achieving these goals. Tech Prep included school-based learning, a work-based component, and connecting activities. It focused on developing students' competencies in broadly defined occupational strands, teaching high school subjects in an applied way, linking high school and college curricula through articulation agreements, and providing opportunities for workplace learning. In 2004, Central Alberta Tech Prep changed its program name to Career Prep to reflect a broader focus on career development. However, Career Prep seems to have been replaced by growing interest in school–college partnerships involving dual credit.

In May 2013, the Alberta government announced funding to support more dual credit programming in schools (O'Donnell, 2013). The proposed dual credit strategy[7] was premised on the notion that labour supply is the biggest impediment to competitiveness in a global, knowledge-based economy. The idea of dual credit was intended, like Tech Prep, to make pathways from high school to college and careers more transparent. As in Ontario, dual credit in Alberta means that a high school student is taking either a high school or a post-secondary course that allows her/him to earn both high school credits and post-secondary credits; the student is registered in the articulated course in both institutions. Prior to the introduction of the official strategy, dual credit initiatives occurred on an ad hoc basis. However, it was seen that more consistent support was needed. At the time of the funding announcement, courses had already been developed with nine post-secondary institutions, including Alberta's two technical institutes (Northern Alberta Institute of Technology and Southern Alberta Institute of Technology). The strategy was intended to build on local practices and to assist school jurisdictions, post-secondary institutions, and partners (including employers) in expanding or creating, delivering, and implementing dual credit programming in their communities. Key actions include engaging more high school students in dual credit programming, investing in student success in dual credit programming, and expanding pathways for high school students.

As in Ontario, some promising initiatives have been introduced in Alberta to help students navigate transitions to post-secondary education and work. However, in terms of student enrolments, the scope of such initiatives is limited, as is the extent to which they affect academic curriculum or increase the status of non-university streams and qualifications. For instance, RAP tends to operate quite separately from the rest of the secondary school program; often students engage in on-the-job training for blocks of time with few formal opportunities to make connections between workplace learning and academic courses (Lehmann & Taylor, 2003). Programs such as Tech Prep attempted to provide parity of esteem for college pathways but there was limited financial investment by government in developing curriculum that would integrate academic and vocational content. It will be interesting to see whether the dual credit initiative will be more successful in this regard. The reliance on employers to drive initiatives usually means that there is little opportunity to place work-based experiences into the larger context, or to critically reflect upon workplace practices.

In addition, competition for students across schools, particularly in urban school districts, tends to increase stratification of school populations based on interests and abilities and runs counter to attempts to unify curriculum. My study of high schools in Edmonton, for example, found a significant degree of differentiation across schools, related to the number of "vocationally oriented" and "university preparation" credits earned (Taylor, 2006b). Further, while school leaders aspired to have strong academic programs, few aspired to having a stronger apprenticeship program, because school reputation and status continued to be tied to university preparation. I discuss high school streaming and its implications further in chapter 6.

The industry-driven nature of school-to-work initiatives in Alberta also has implications. While it ensures a better match with available work, it fails to promote the kind of progressive vocationalism espoused by Dewey and other critical writers (Kincheloe, 1999; Simon, Dippo, & Schenke, 1991). Rather, it aims to prepare disaffected young people for the disciplines of the workplace, as a member of the Legislative Assembly who participated in developing the *Framework for Enhancing Business Involvement in Education* suggests:

> When you talk to business people and you ask them, what is the number one reason why new employees, particularly those straight out of high school, lose their first job? And the answer will be, it's not because they can't read or write or count . . . it's that they have no work ethic. They have no values and attitudes that promote things like working together; they can't get along. They can't work in teams. They don't have any pride in workmanship. They don't care how much materials they waste or tools they break. They don't care to show up on time. . . .That's why I think involvement of business can in fact highlight the value and

importance of having appropriate values and attitudes. (Cited in Taylor, 2002, 61)

From this perspective, school-to-work transition initiatives adopt a functionalist approach: they are about socializing young people to the existing workplace. This is quite different from the worker-centred view, described by a representative from organized labour in Alberta:

> We support public education not to make us into better workers, but to open the world to us. (Cited in Lehmann & Taylor, 2003, p. 59)

A broader view of vocational education and training would encourage youth to critically reflect on what they are doing and to locate their work within a wider context of values (Hager & Hyland, 2003; Pring, 2004). In contrast, employer-driven VET is more likely to result in an "excessive preoccupation with the immediacies of the work environment" (Skillbeck, Connell, Lowe, & Tait, 1994). Moreover, in Alberta employer-driven VET tends to result in focus on areas of immediate labour demand (particularly in the energy sector).

There is also a question of whether private–public partnerships are likely to promote equitable distribution of outcomes by gender, social background, and region. In both Ontario and Alberta, evidence suggests that youth apprenticeship and other school-to-work initiatives continue to be highly gender segregated. In addition, levels of parental education among youth apprentices are lower than among those in university tracks (Taylor, Lehmann, Raykov, & Hamm, 2013). Although politicians usually justify vocational education initiatives in terms of better outcomes for "youth at risk," there has been little tracking of these outcomes by governments; accordingly, questions arise regarding social mobility versus social reproduction. Chapters 5 and 6 address questions around equity in greater depth.

Concluding Comments

> At the political-economy level, who influences the goals of the education system and to what ends and, at a material level, who pays for what types of educational provision are areas of potential contestation between different parties to the process. (Gleeson & Keep, 2004, p 38)

In their discussion of vocational education in England since the mid 1990s, Denis Gleeson and Ewart Keep (2004) raise concerns about the undue influence of employers. This influence is problematic, in their view, because employers' interests are often in conflict with those of students and teachers—employers generally promote a narrow, utilitarian vision of the purpose of education. Further, economic changes and employer diversity means that there is a cacophony of conflicting voices about the skills needed. Gleeson and Keep recommend clearer articulation of the roles and responsibilities of all stakeholders in VET, so that employers are both more accountable and more responsible for education. They would like to see unions, as representatives of worker interests, be granted a more active role, and suggest that employer demands be placed in a wider civic perspective.

This discussion has relevance for the Canadian context where, as in the UK, a voluntaristic system of VET places faith in employers to step up in large numbers and provide high-quality training for youth. The examples of Ontario and Alberta highlight this "market" approach to SWT. Since the late 1980s, school–business partnerships have been seen as a way to revitalize vocational education in light of trends that include declining enrolments in old "tech" courses, lack of capacity of schools to provide high-quality training in-house because of cost-cutting, and increasing investment in digital technologies as school priorities shift toward increasing students' digital literacy. My research suggests that while VET initiatives can be perceived by youth as valuable, results tend to be uneven because of a lack of regulation of training, the disproportionate influence of employers (vis-à-vis students and teachers), and lack of involvement of worker representatives (e.g., unions) (Taylor, 2002; 2005; Taylor, Lehmann, & Raykov, 2014). Unsurprisingly, training is provided in areas of immediate employer need, with less attention to a more expansive vision of vocationalization as part of education for life, requiring broadly defined skills and knowledge that are valuable both now and in the future (Skillbeck, Connell, Lowe, & Tait, 1994). Further, attempts to increase the value of secondary schooling for students run up against the ways in which skills and credentials act to unequally structure positions within society (Brown, 2000). Therefore, I share concerns about the market direction of vocationalization in schooling.

While school–business partnerships have been a priority since the 1990s, growing concerns about NEETs and PINEs may be responsible for the more recent trend in Canada and the US toward school–college partnerships, particularly the growth of dual credit initiatives that seek to better articulate high school and college curricula. These partnerships are still in their infancy, with government, schools, and colleges working out practical issues. In an economy where more and more youth are seeking post-secondary qualifications, this direction will potentially expand the horizons of action for some youth, while raising the quality and status of vocational education. However, the history of vocationalism in Canada and in many other countries directs our attention to a few considerations. First, if the idea is to provide more flexible pathways with opportunities for youth to change direction, then articulation efforts should focus on "vocational–academic" program articulation and transfer to avoid the continuing separation of educational pathways. Relatedly, if the goal is to break down dualistic ideas about theory/practice and head/hand, then the reform focus should be on all curricula, not only "technology" courses. In chapter 5, I further discuss the need to challenge academic–vocational division, with reference to research on apprentices' learning.

Finally, the idea of moving from school–business partnerships to school–community partnerships seems to be taking hold in some places, and provides potential for a more civic-minded vocationalism to develop. Reasons for broadening school partnerships beyond business include the current challenges in finding sufficient numbers of high-quality off-campus placements for students, the desirability of encouraging students to consider a wide range of career options, and the movement of much vocational training to colleges. In education–community partnerships, experiential learning opportunities are provided for high school and PSE students to learn about and contribute to their communities (e.g., Council of Ontario Universities, 2014). A number of provincial education ministries already ask high school students to contribute to their community for a specified number of hours as a requirement of graduation. However, these activities are often poorly integrated with the rest of students' programs, are poorly monitored, and lack meaning for students. Yet, off-campus experiential learning in universities, for example, in community service–learning, has been shown to yield benefits for students that go beyond instrumental "learning for earning" aims (Westheimer & Kahne, 2004). These initiatives could arguably be better integrated with other parts of student programs to develop valuable connective learning experiences.

Chapter 5

The Relationship between Everyday and Theoretical Knowledge

I don't see a hell of a lot of difference in [my sister and her friends who attend university and myself] other than they basically have to sit down and learn everything that they know, and I get to stand up and learn everything I know. . . . I'm learning every day on the job. (Interview, heavy equipment operator and former high school apprentice, Alberta)[1]

Previous chapters document the historical rise of vocational education in Canada and the recent development of programs aimed at smoothing youth transitions to work in Ontario and Alberta. Vocational education programs in North American schools have long been associated with working-class youth and reflect the lower status of occupations constructed more as "manual" than "mental." Recent reports indicate that differential access to valued knowledge for working-class and minoritized youth persists (Clanfield et al., 2014).

However, the popular idea that national economic competitiveness in the current "knowledge economy" is tied more to the skills and creative capacities of all workers than it has been in the past raises questions about lingering academic–vocational and mental–manual divisions. It also raises questions more generally about the ability of "industrial age" curriculum to prepare youth for future work. As noted in chapter 4, policy initiatives associated with new vocationalism aim to blur the lines between academic and vocational curricula. Yet, my research on high school apprenticeship reveals that youth apprentices perceive little attempt to make connections between their learning in the high school classroom and their learning in the workplace. This research also suggests that these apprentices have been constructed (and construct themselves) as "hands-on" learners rather than book learners. Moreover, they are aware of the perceived lower status of their occupational choices. Thus, divisions and struggles over access to and control of different forms of knowledge are still with us today.

This chapter stems from my belief that the organization of knowledge in high schools is a critical topic of debate, and that issues such as streaming and the specific knowledge required to prepare youth for work warrant close examination. I explore the legacy of ideas about the relationship between theoretical and everyday knowledge, beginning with Aristotle and Plato, before addressing contemporary visions for vocational education and training.

The History of Vocational Education and Occupational Status Hierarchy

> The devaluation of vocational education is predicated on the problematic metaphysical mind/body distinction and the epistemic hierarchy it effects in academic discourse. Rationalist epistemologies, such as those embodied in Platonic and Cartesian philosophy, privilege the mind as the source of immutable truth and understanding and condemn the body as the source of irrational appetite, sensory error, and moral instability. (Hyslop-Margison, 2001)

Chapter 3 refers briefly to debates in the early twentieth century over whether instrumental skills-based education or traditional academic programs better prepare students for their occupational life. In 1914, US President Woodrow Wilson appointed a commission to study the need for federal aid to vocational education. Charles Prosser, a student of social efficiency advocate David Snedden, was the principal author of the commission's report to Congress (Hyslop-Margison, 2001).[2] Prosser and Snedden supported self-administered, narrowly focused, and mandatory vocational education to help non-academic students secure intermediate employment after completing school. Snedden believed that it made little sense to expose the majority of students to comprehensive high school curricula, blaming their early departure from school on their inability to understand abstract subject matter.

In contrast, John Dewey believed that vocational education should be included as part of a comprehensive curriculum to help students develop a greater range of personal capacities that expand rather than limit their future occupational options. He rejected an image of students as passive individuals, controlled by market economy forces and limited by their inherent intellectual capacities (Hyslop-Margison, 2001). Instead, he embraced a progressive approach to develop industrial intelligence in youth, which would be based on knowledge of social problems and conditions. Dewey felt that the best liberal education was vocational and the best vocational education was liberal (Young, 1998).

The Snedden–Prosser side of the debate supports the argument that the status of vocational education and its purposes and practices have been rooted in assumptions about the capacities of different workers and acceptance of an occupational hierarchy that constructs a division between head and hand, privileging mental over manual work. The ideological foundations for a "status-laden and cognitively inflected distinction among kinds of work" go back to early Western thought (Rose, 2012, p. 9). For example, in *The Republic*, Plato argues that the soul of the craftsman is "warped and maimed," and in his *Politics*, Aristotle proposes that artisans and merchants be denied citizenship because their work is "ignoble and inimical to goodness" (cited in Rose, 2012, pp. 9–10). During antiquity, the institution of slavery represented an attempt to exclude labour from the conditions of man's life, according to Hannah Arendt (1958). Contempt for labouring arose out of a passionate striving for freedom from necessity. The "meanest occupations" were described by Aristotle as those "in which the body is most deteriorated" (cited in Arendt, pp. 81–82). Thus, from early times, the division between "liberal" and "servile" arts was political.

The effect of this hierarchical valuing became evident in the preparation for different kinds of work in more recent times. For example, liberal university education in the UK and other European countries was charged with the task of preparing (usually male) students from relatively privileged backgrounds for employment in the clergy, public service, or diplomacy (Billett, 2014). In contrast, preparation for occupations with low standing and perceived limited requirements was accomplished through specific, short-term training provisions. Various writers have argued that the distinction between a "profession" and a "job" reflects societally imposed distinctions related to the power of different occupational groups rather than informed comparisons of different work requirements (Collins, 1979). An example is the successful pressure from employer associations in Australia to reduce the time required for trades training since 1945, while the extent of education and training required for new professions has stayed the same or increased (Billett, 2014).

Occupational status thus reflects power relations in society. For example, the Hope-Goldthorpe Scale depicts a hierarchy of occupations' social desirability that continues to reflect the differential valuing of mental and manual work that Plato proposed centuries ago (Billett, 2014). This scale provides a continuum from class 1 (including professionals, managers, and administrators) to class 7 (semi-skilled and unskilled manual workers). Interestingly, routine non-manual work (associated with class 3) is viewed as more socially desirable than manual work. This kind of valuing is also implicit in qualifications frameworks developed in Australia and Europe.

Writers such as Mike Rose (2012) and Richard Sennett (2008) challenge the value assumptions that underlie these typologies, partly on the basis that they ignore the intimate connection between hand and head that is part of "craftsmanship"—broadly defined as the desire and ability to do a job well for its own sake. This quality of craftsmanship, which can be exhibited by workers ranging from carpenters and lab technicians to orchestra conductors and surgeons, requires a high degree of skill developed through higher-order capacities involving problem finding and problem solving. Sennett (2008) suggests that the dialogue between head and hand is evident in common phrases about learning such as "coming to grips with an issue" or "grasping something" (p. 151). Further, practical knowledge continues to evolve because specific practices prepare the ground on which people can make intuitive leaps.

Skills begin as bodily process and are refined through practice. Sennett argues that in order to build and expand skills there must be an open relationship between problem solving and problem finding. Borrowing from C. Wright Mills, he suggests that craft work is characterized by the connection between the worker's daily labour and end product, the ability to control one's own actions at work, the freedom to experiment, and engagement with work in and for itself. Ideally, in Sennett's model, workers' knowledge and skills expand and work processes evolve. Michael Polanyi similarly problematizes the theory–practice divide, arguing that tacit thought forms an indispensable part of all knowledge. In his 1966 book *Tacit Knowledge*, Polanyi argues that a true knowledge of theory can be established only after it has been interiorized and extensively used to interpret experience. Tacit knowledge joins two levels of knowledge—knowledge about the particular (proximal knowledge) and more comprehensive knowledge about organizing principles (distal knowledge). The dialectical interplay between the two levels is how knowledge evolves.

Relating this discussion to vocational education, Mike Rose (2012) problematizes the idea that rote learning is the best way to address the low motivation of students in vocational and remedial education courses at community colleges. In more affirming language, he describes a student in a welding class as follows:

> Tommy is engaged in intense self-monitoring and analysis of his performance and significant intellectual work in applying what he's been learning to the task in front of him. It's hard to know where to mark the Cartesian separation between body and mind. Touch and concept blend in activity. Of course, as Tommy masters his trade, his response to the dynamic variability he describes will become second nature. We typically use words like "routine" and "automatic" to describe this level of expertise, but I think that vocabulary erroneously suggests that at a point in development, mind fades from physical performance. It's true that constant monitoring does diminish, but not mindfulness and not that fusion of touch and concept, as you'll see in welding, or hairstyling, or heart surgery when something goes wrong. Suddenly attention is focused, and all kinds of knowledge rush in on the moment, right through the fingertips. (p. 9)

Rose thus observes the interplay between kinesthetic experience and thought in this kind of learning. The term *absorbed concentration* is thus a better descriptor than "mindless routine" for Tommy's process of skill development.

Acknowledging the interconnected ideological, structural, and symbolic dimensions of the academic–vocational divide, Rose argues that its assumptions about learners have the effect of narrowing our understanding of human cognition and constraining our pedagogical imagination. There has been pressure on vocational teachers to emphasize job-specific skills to the near exclusion of theoretical content, or to assume that educational reforms should focus only on "vocational" curriculum, leaving academic knowledge untouched.

Instead of assuming that youth who gravitate toward work-based learning cannot understand abstract concepts, it may be more useful to think about how they learn. Unfortunately, formal schooling in Western societies tends to privilege generalization and decontextualization, the ability to move away from the particular (Vadeboncoeur & Collie, 2013). However, Mjelde (1987) suggests that students should be given opportunities to move from practice to theory rather than this dominant approach. When students are offered theory in relation to practice, they are more likely to understand complex problems and solutions.

However, the legacy of a divisive approach to academic and vocational education was evident in our interviews with high school apprentices, where those who had been constructed as "academic" were often seen by trainers as lacking "hand skills" while others who excelled in the "shop" class were failing math tests (Taylor & Watt-Malcolm, 2007). As Mjelde writes, everyone suffers from the division of theory and practice.

The Effects of Academic–Vocational Division in High School

Nancy Jackson (1993) suggests that ideas about learning for work have been constructed historically as a form of "education for other people's children." Stephen Billett (2014) adds that the voices of students are rarely taken into account in vocational education policy. His own research tries to address this problem, suggesting that students enter vocational education programs for a wide variety of reasons and exercise discretion in the educational process—they are agentic rather than passive. Our research[3] into high school apprenticeship programs in Ontario and Alberta supports the importance of including student voices in policy discussions.

Our studies aimed to learn more about the high school and post-graduation experiences of youth apprentices in two provinces. The findings of these studies challenge common assumptions about learners in vocational education programs—for instance, the assumption that these programs are mostly populated by disaffected learners who need to engage in routine tasks because they are incapable of more. Contra this assumption, we found that although high school apprentices were left largely on their own to make connections between their high school and on-the-job learning, they valued the classroom portion of trades training as a necessary complement to their workplace learning. The majority described themselves as lifelong learners whose idea of a "good job" was related as much to knowledge-expansion opportunities as to financial rewards. Further, while many researchers have noted the lower status of trades training vis-à-vis university education, the apprentices' accounts challenged this value hierarchy (Lehmann, Taylor, & Wright, 2014).

Students in high school apprenticeship programs in Alberta usually complete the hours for the first year of their apprenticeship and gain high school credits at the same time. But few of the 56 former high school apprentices interviewed in Alberta saw a connection between their academic classroom learning and on-the-job apprenticeship training. An electrician (formerly in the Registered Apprenticeship Program, or RAP) commented that, "It was like night and day, it really was." RAP is usually an add-on to the high school experience, whereby students attend school for certain parts of the day, days of the week, or even alternate semesters and learn on the job as apprentices at other times. Teachers of academic courses are usually not aware of apprentices' out-of-school activities, and high school coordinators who monitor off-campus programs often lack the requisite knowledge of apprenticeship training to properly support youth.

As former high school apprentices reflect back on their academic performance in high school, most acknowledge that they struggled. When asked how they learn best, almost all describe themselves as "hands-on" learners. But when pressed, it became clear that a large part of this learning style involved their need to see a connection between what they were learning from books or teachers and their practical activities in the world. As Luria (cited in Mjelde, 1987) suggests, while the average middle-class child solves a problem by first talking about it and then acting, working-class children are more inclined to solve a problem by acting and then talking about it. While this may be overly simplistic, it seems logical that young people's approaches to learning are shaped by their early socialization experiences.

For example, a hairdressing apprentice recalled that her favourite classes in high school were auto mechanics and cosmetology because the experiences did not involve "sitting in a classroom staring at a chalk-board and reading books all the time; it was actually getting out and doing stuff." Similarly, a female mechanic commented, "anyone can read a book from front to back, but it's putting what you learned into use" that is important. Comments from a third participant, a heavy-duty mechanic, suggest that this preference for "connective knowledge" is perhaps a more important distinction than being a "hands-on" versus a "book" learner:

Q: *What's a typical workday like for you?*
I get to work at 5:30, drink some coffee. I get told what to do and if I can't figure out the problem, I go to books that give you diagnoses and troubleshooting trees and stuff like that. I'll try this. If that doesn't work, I try that.

The idea of *connective knowledge* makes clear the vocational aspects of academic subject knowledge and recognizes that learning is a purposive and social process that takes place explicitly or implicitly in a community of practice with other learners (Young, 1998).

Other apprentices in our research referred to "success" not only in terms of material rewards, but also in terms of solving problems at work, learning new things, and becoming as "smart" as respected colleagues on the worksite. In fact, the contrast between their descriptions of their high school learning and subsequent learning was stark. For example, consider the following excerpts from interviews with apprentices working in a variety of trades:

Q: *You didn't like school, but do you like learning?*
I do like learning. I love learning new things. That's one of my favorite things to do. (Electrician)

Further, a youth who described high school classrooms as "kind of tedious," describes other learning contexts more positively:

Q: *How important is learning on the job to you?*
Very important.

Q: *Do you find the in-school [trades] training valuable?*
Oh yeah, it's pretty valuable. It teaches you a lot. You learn new stuff in school that you wouldn't really know, stuff that you wouldn't see on the job every day. (Sheet metal trade)

Q: *How do you define success?*
In the work, if I'm getting a job that I've never done before, never seen before. If . . . I can figure it out, that's success. . . .

Q: *What do you like most about the work?*
The troubleshooting, and there's always something new to learn. (Instrument technician)

Q: *Did you go to different worksites in order to keep learning?*
Yeah. . . . I want to learn the whole circle of this trade. I've got the heavy duty, I got the ATV [all terrain vehicle] and entertainment. I want the lightweight vehicles. (Parts technician)

Most of the youth valued the classroom learning that was required to become certified in their trade because it provided knowledge that was relevant but unavailable on the worksite. For example, when asked to compare his trades training in class and on the job, an electrician replied:

On the job, you're pulling wire, you're hooking it up. Your meters tell you everything. You read the panel door and it tells you what the voltage is and stuff like that. But you get into the schooling and they teach you, what if the motor didn't have a nameplate on, could you still identify that motor? . . . Could you figure out the theory behind how they got that information on the nameplate?

Thus, while many preferred to learn on the job, they recognize the value of theoretical knowledge. Further, most saw themselves as motivated lifelong learners. The following two excerpts demonstrate the enthusiasm expressed by youth about the alternation between classroom and workplace learning during apprenticeship training:

Right now I feel like I'm learning every day. I go to work and I learn something new. Even the littlest things sometimes can surprise you. Like the other day I was working on a valve set and my foreman came up to me and said, "how do you set the valves, a little bit tight or a little bit loose?" I said, "well I guess on the tighter side, for wear." He said, "well think about this—what wears the most?" I said, "I don't know." He said, "well basically what I want to know is where has the most cheat and least lubrication?" I said, "I don't know, the valve head?" He's like, "yeah exactly." He said, "think about it. As the valve heads wear, what's going to happen?" I'm like, oh, that kind of makes sense. They actually get tighter, so you actually want to set it on the loose side. It's not so important that it matters, like it doesn't really matter. You're not going to get that much extended life out of it. But the point is that just knowing that that's where it wears is kind of interesting. Then I had this urge to tell somebody else about that. (Heavy equipment operator)

Similarly, a chef spoke in glowing terms about his training at a technical college:

It was absolutely amazing. I could've challenged my exam.[4] . . . [but] I wanted to go to school to actually learn this stuff. The chef I had for my first year, I think every first year cook should have. This man had passion I've never seen before. He's really French, really old school. He can solve any problem with butter, bacon or white wine, guaranteed. He was really passionate, really savvy. He allowed us a lot of freedom. . . . He really just kind of pushed us as chefs as opposed to cooks, which was great. Then the second year . . . [college] poached the city's top three chefs to teach the apprenticeship program. . . . So it turns out I got [name of instructor and restaurant] . . . they're sort of spearheading slow food and field to table cooking. As far as I'm concerned,

I think that's the way the world of food needs to move. . . . It was really cool just having that perspective. Also, having a chef who's fresh out of industry. He's a little less stiff backed about it and he's got a lot of current, up to date experience. . . . On top of that, the school had just opened a garden on-site. It was absolutely amazing to go down and walk through a garden and pick my own things. It's just like the most overwhelming blossoming of passion I've ever had. Just being there really changed the way I look at food.

These positive comments reinforce the importance of both classroom and on-the-job training. Other youth added that apprenticeship training was just the beginning of their learning, noting the importance of continuing to ask questions of experienced mentors and pursuing further training. Several participants (more young men than women) aspired to own a business and were committed to learning as much as they could about their RAP trade and others to prepare for that goal. But again, much of this learning was informal, as this millwright, who started a business in his early twenties, recounts:

My partner was five years older. We didn't know anything about [starting a business]. We bought a tax software program. You need to have an invoice and you need to have business cards. It was very rudimentary. We knew we had work. . . . Then you go and buy insurance, set up a WCB account, and all that stuff. Pay into it all. . . . After we got everything arranged, we went to work, and that was it.

In sum, apprentices valued the alternation between formal and informal learning that characterized their training. However, some participants felt that the standards for assessing trades knowledge were too low and their capabilities were not necessarily recognized in written trades examinations. For example, the same chef whose passion was ignited in trade school was disappointed with the government exam that tested his knowledge:

I came out of my first year exam angry, just angry. Now talking to [instructor at college] this year we realized there's a reason for some of it. . . . I came, I paid, I worked, I studied. This is the first time in my entire educational career that I said, I'm going to sit down and study for four hours, and did. I enjoyed it. I sat down with my friends and we had flash cards. But I learned my five mother sauces and derivative sauces and the primal cuts on a cow and all these things that your average cook doesn't know; they've been told what the job wants them to know and how to do it. But I can walk into work and say, oh you know, today I feel like making a red beet soufflé. . . . I have this knowledge. And I get to my government exam and I get asked multiple choice, what side of the grilled cheese should you butter when preparing a grilled cheese—outside, inside, both sides, no sides? I'm like, really? This is what I need to know to be a chef in the industry? One of my mentors in my kitchen . . . I remember when he wrote his Red Seal exam, same thing. He came in and he was just livid the day after. I was like, why? He's like, you tell me, what's the traditional preparation for nachos? You're kidding.

Similarly, a former apprentice in Ontario suggested that his high school pre-apprenticeship course involved problematic assumptions about the academic abilities about youth who choose trades. For example:

[Y]ou know how Ontario has the . . . *academic*, and *college* and *workplace* [course streams in high school], I felt that the pre-apprenticeship course was like below workplace and it was very, like, "Okay kids, this is what we're going to be doing, you guys are the apprenticeship students." And . . . it felt very dumbed down which, it was not necessary . . . just 'cause we're interested in auto mechanics doesn't mean I'm incapable of reading . . . you felt like a dummy in [OYAP]. (Taylor, Lehmann, & Raykov, 2014)

At the same time, the main basis for evaluating apprenticeship training is written tests.

Michael Young (1998) suggests that low-status knowledge tends to be characterized by oral presentation, group activities and assessment, concreteness of the knowledge involved, and its relatedness to non-school knowledge, while high-status knowledge is characterized by written literacy, individualism, abstractness, and lack of relatedness to everyday experience. The ideological power of the latter lies in its ability to convince people that it is the only way of organizing knowledge to develop students' intellectual capabilities and that those who do not succeed are in-educable.

However, the accounts of apprentices suggest that the failure to help students to successfully integrate theory and practice in their learning processes is problematic. For example, an instrument technician who had the grades to enrol in engineering at university but decided to pursue a trade suggests that the typical way of learning in academic courses is different but no more challenging than learning in practice:

> I was maybe a little stuck up about [trade school]—I just did [university entrance courses in my final year of high school]. [I thought] it's trade school; it'll be easy. Then I went in and it's just a different way of thinking. I wasn't prepared for that kind of way of thinking. It's more mechanical. As much as I liked using my hands, I'd never really had to think about the mechanics of something, how this is going to work. This is going to do this and this is going to do that. So I was kind of taken aback when I got to school. Oh my God, I'm going to have to work at this, it's not going to be a piece of cake. I was taken by surprise by how difficult it is. It was way more challenging than I expected, but it worked out well. I worked at it and I got it, so that was good. Each year it progressed and I got better and felt more comfortable. It became easier to me, that kind of way of thinking, using that part of my brain.

But youth who chose trades found that their training did not articulate well with university studies. For example, a few apprentices expressed interest in going to university for engineering but admitted that the upgrading required to get into programs would be prohibitive. This appears to be related to the devaluation of practical knowledge and differences in values and pedagogical approaches in academic and vocational courses. The school system encourages students to aspire to higher education and tends to denigrate work associated with manual labour. Further, while the values of equal treatment, moral obligation, and comradeship tend to characterize vocational training, values of competition and individualism are more prevalent in academic studies (Mjelde, 1987). A rich vision of vocational education and knowledge supports the development of a fairer and more just society in which everyone's capabilities and talents are celebrated (Hayward, 2004). Finally, ways of presenting knowledge and the priority given to different types of knowledge differ in trades education versus in university studies.

Rethinking Education

Current economic trends undermine the economic and social division of labour on which tracked systems, rooted in the industrial revolutions of their respective countries are based. They create a demand for *higher levels and new types of skills and knowledge,* especially generic and overarching competences, and for their wide distribution across the workforce. (Raffe et al., 1998) [emphasis added]

The above quote from UK researchers echoes the popular idea that the knowledge economy requires new kinds of knowledge and new vocational approaches, which challenge the practice of tracking students into "academic" or "vocational" programs. But "new vocational" discourse is not all that new. Polytechnical education was proposed by Karl Marx more than a century ago, as a way of promoting the full development of all young people by combining theory and practice and challenging class-based divisions of labour (Mjelde, 1987).

In the 1990s, "one of the most significant developments in educational policy" was the drive to unify post-compulsory education and training systems (Raffe et al., 1998). Several European countries introduced education reforms aimed at bringing different curriculum tracks into closer alignment. Reform strategies include the development of *linked* systems intended to provide possibilities for student transfer and parity of esteem for vocational and general tracks, and the establishment of a *unified* system that abolishes formal status differences by eliminating tracks. Consistent with Dewey's vision, a unified curriculum would not separate the preparation of young people for employment from the wider role of preparing them to become democratic citizens (Young, 1998). But there has been resistance to a unified system in the UK because it challenges the existing social order and powerful interests (Raffe et al., 1998; Young, 1998). Therefore, the tendency has been to try to reform vocational curriculum with little change to academic curriculum.

Canadian education systems tend to be more open than systems in the UK, France, and Germany; "Canadian schools have largely promoted 'practical' curricula and have not equated 'excellence' and 'quality' with high culture" (Davies & Guppy, 2014, p. 94). Still, my discussion in chapter 4 suggests that neo-liberal educational reforms, particularly increased emphasis on competition and choice and reliance on voluntary vocational education partnerships, can work against "open systems" by promoting and maintaining stratification across schools. Further, our study of data from the 2000 "Youth in Transition Survey," which included 15-year-olds across Canada, found that although high school streaming (or tracking) has become less deterministic than in the past—with students being streamed by course rather than by program—parents' education and income continue to impact youth outcomes (Taylor & Krahn, 2009).

Vocational streaming in schools is also common, although it is difficult to monitor, given that "vocational" courses are usually optional.

But taking high school apprenticeship programs as an example, we know that only a small proportion of students participate, that programs tend to be highly gendered, and that a higher proportion of students from working-class than from middle-class backgrounds participate (Taylor et al., 2013). The inequitable implications of streaming are discussed in more detail in chapter 6. Further, many youth who have participated in these programs (such as those cited above) do not feel that they have been well served by the academic–vocational division that they have experienced in compulsory and post-compulsory education. A carpentry apprentice argues for opportunities to combine qualifications as follows:

> You take two people . . . one's taking a college course and one's taking a university course. And yeah, the university course, they know everything in depth, but the person in college has the experience. They have more application. So mixing it together is definitely the thing to do. (Cited in Taylor & Freeman, 2011)

The concept of *hybrid qualifications* (HQ) is becoming popular in Europe (Deissinger, Aff, Fuller, & Jorgensen, 2013). Such qualifications result from education–training pathways that provide access to both employment and higher education, either through an integrated curriculum in a single program (integrative HQ) or through earning vocational and general qualifications separately (additive HQ) (Helms Jorgensen, 2010). In countries such as Germany, it makes sense that hybrid qualifications are aimed more at youth who have been streamed at an early age into vocational education programs. In Canada's more open system, such initiatives tend to be aimed more at shifting the high aspirations of youth so that they consider pursuing non-university technical programs in which they can develop the intermediate skills demanded in the labour market (Taylor, Watt-Malcolm, & Wimmer, 2013).

Initiatives such as Tech Prep in Alberta and Applied Academics in British Columbia (introduced in the 1990s),[5] and the more recent School–College Work Initiative in Ontario and dual credit in Alberta attempt to break down barriers between theory and practice. They aim to improve articulation between high school and college curricula, just as International Baccalaureate (IB) and Advanced Placement (AP) programs prepare students for university studies. But both Tech Prep and Applied Academics had short lifespans. Moreover, neither had any effect on university preparation programs, which continue to be more attractive to schools and students, and more resistant to change (Taylor, 2006a). In the UK too, efforts to reform the academic "A level" curriculum since the 1960s have failed because of a lack of clear alternatives and strong opposition (Young, 1998).

The difficulty in breaking down divisions between academic and vocational education (and between theory and practice) is rooted partly in resistance from middle-class parents. But it is clear from the discussion above that the devaluation of practical education and manual occupations has a long history. While simple solutions are elusive, it may be fruitful to consider changes in the pedagogy and curriculum within vocational programs that will enhance their value. For example, helping students to integrate their learning in school and at work might help students make connections between theoretical and practical knowledge (Guile & Young, 2003).

My research with co-investigators into high school apprenticeship in Ontario and Alberta suggests that youth are poorly served when there is a disconnect between school and work learning, when limiting assumptions are made about students' abilities and motivations to learn "academic material," and when on-the-job learning is assumed to be sufficient for student learning. Most apprentices saw little relation between their learning on the job and in school because these activities were separated both materially and conceptually. Although high school apprentices received cooperative education credits with the expectation that they would have opportunities to reflect on their learning at work during "integration days," the reality was quite different (Taylor & Watt-Malcolm, 2008)—there was little integration of learning, and the crossing of boundaries between school and work was left largely up to students.

It was also assumed that students participating in apprenticeship were "hands-on learners" who had no time for formal learning, especially theory. However, as noted above, this is far from the reality expressed by these students. Although, as Mjelde (1987) suggests, apprentices preferred to move from practice to theory, most saw the value of the latter. By way of example, our study recorded the following conversation between two carpentry apprentices:

Apprentice 1: I don't know why we need the geometry [at this level].

Apprentice 2: No, like remember when we were doing the ellipses? And [name of teacher] took us over into the shop and he showed us how to do that.

Apprentice 1: Isn't that for, what, the finishing people?

Apprentice 2: It's also for rough work, like say cutting a hole on a roof . . . if you have like a circle, like, you have to put a pipe through and it's on a slant, it's not going to be a circle, it's going to be an ellipse. And you have to know how to calculate that so it fits nicely. (Cited in Taylor & Watt-Malcolm, 2007, p. 35)

This exchange suggests the importance of integrating theory and practice, and the value of the former. Learning on the job is often not sufficient, not only because students do not gain a full understanding of how knowledge about work process evolves but also because workplaces can have a restrictive effect on apprentices' learning. More attention to learning that connects classroom and workplace is needed so that more apprentices experience the ideal of the craftsman described by Sennett (2008).

Based on their extensive research into apprenticeship in the UK, Alison Fuller and Lorna Unwin (2006) define a continuum of *expansive* and *restrictive* training contexts. Expansive contexts support the learning and development of apprentices by exposing them to learning experiences across the company, giving them access to a range of qualifications and qualified mentors, supporting them to take time off for reflection and theoretical instruction, and generally mentoring them in their transition from outsider to full/expert participant. On the other hand, in restrictive contexts, access to learning is more limited in terms of tasks, knowledge, and location. In addition, there are few opportunities for reflection, and apprentices are expected to transition quickly to become productive employees. Unfortunately, our studies of high school apprentices have found that, while most workplaces have some expansive and some restrictive features (there is a continuum), restrictive learning contexts are not uncommon. Given that schools are relying more on employers to provide off-campus vocational training, as opposed to providing it in-house, more oversight must be given by schools to the quality of this training.

In addition, vocational education programs could be enhanced if the development of practical knowledge and the actual experiences of youth moving between school and work become a more central focus. In an article called "Transfer and Transition in Vocational Education," David Guile and Michael Young (2003) challenge the idea of knowledge transfer as a one-way mechanical process in which students acquire employability skills in vocational schooling and apply them in the workplace in an unproblematic way. Guile and Young draw on a socio-cultural research tradition that sees the acquisition of skills as a social process involving participation by learners in new contexts (see also Jackson, 1993). Rather than decontextualized and static, knowledge is viewed as inseparable from the questions of *who* knows it and *how* they use it (i.e., from issues of power and identity). It follows that knowledge transfer involves changes in individuals' identities.

Guile and Young call for new types of learning relationships between teachers, instructors, and students in schools and workplaces. In these relationships, students would be encouraged to identify the mismatches they experience between what they need to know as trainees and what they need to know in employment, and teachers would do more to support students in relating their "situated" knowledge of workplaces to the codified knowledge of the curriculum. In other words, the boundary-crossing between school and work, between theory and practice, would become a key focus of the inquiry.

My studies of high school apprentices suggest that connective learning would improve experiences and outcomes for youth. It would challenge the academic–vocational dichotomy and raise the status of work-based programs by demonstrating the value of practical knowledge. Further, it would challenge students in "vocational" programs in ways that acknowledge and validate their backgrounds and abilities. Moreover, it would move in the direction of an education-led economy, rather than an economy-led education system (cf. Young, 1998).

Chapter 6

Rethinking Vocational Education and "Youth at Risk"

My own father and mother immigrated to Canada from Glasgow, Scotland, after World War II. My dad was a cabinetmaker by trade, having left school at age 15 to begin an apprenticeship with his father's firm.[1] He would have liked to continue his schooling but was not given the option (he enjoyed academics and I attribute my interest in education partly to his vicarious interest in my schooling). Despite leaving formal education at a young age, my dad was a dedicated lifelong learner—he read extensively, wrote short stories throughout his adult life, and when in his sixties, successfully completed a senior secondary school course in English by correspondence. I remember this achievement being very meaningful to him. My mother, coming from a large working-class family, also left school for work at age 14. She worked in "unskilled" jobs for the duration of her paid work life, in Scotland and later in Canada. Disheartened by the often precarious nature of their work, both of my parents wanted "something better" for my brother and me.

Using today's language, I would be classified as a "first-gen" student—the first in their family to attend university. There is growing interest in how to support working-class students in post-secondary education, due to the recognition that they have much lower odds of attending university than youth from families with university-educated parents (Lehmann, 2012). Statistically, the odds of attending university are also lower for some racialized groups and for males, although overall, men still fare better in terms of labour-market returns (McInturff, 2013).

Despite growing concerns about the declining labour-market returns of a university degree vis-à-vis other forms of post-compulsory education (discussed in chapter 2), university credentials continue to be equated with better life chances.

The preceding chapters examined the historical development of vocational education at the secondary school level in Canada. Chapter 5 challenged the division between academic and vocational education, questioning the taken-for-granted hierarchy of knowledge and proposing an alternative understanding of the relationship between theoretical and practical knowledge. This chapter confronts the academic–vocational division on the basis of its inequitable effects on youth. Here, I raise the social justice question: Which groups of youth have access to what kinds of knowledge? In answer, I discuss research indicating how streaming perpetuates inequities based on social class, gender, race/ethnicity, (dis)ability, and geographic location—for example, working-class youth continue to be directed to paths leading to working-class work (see also Clanfield et al., 2014; King et al., 2009; Parekh, Killoran, & Crawford, 2011; Taylor & Krahn, 2009).

Further, I challenge the assumption that work-based education is inferior and thus all students should aspire to a university education. It is true that, as currently structured, work-based education programs in secondary schools (e.g., youth apprenticeship programs) tend to provide less support for students than university preparation programs such as Advanced Placement and International Baccalaureate (Taylor, 2006a). But this situation reflects historical legacies and the persistent undervaluing of these programs in Canada—it does not have to be this way.[2] My argument is that academic streaming (which plays a role in determining future work opportunities) adversely affects all students, and that all youth would benefit from more integrated formal and informal work-based learning opportunities through their compulsory and post-compulsory schooling.

In response to concerns about youth transitions to work, including anxiety around job–skills mismatch, provincial ministries of education have tried to make the educational requirements for different career pathways more transparent. They have introduced high school apprenticeship programs to address labour shortages in trades and other *intermediate skills* occupations, and to encourage parity of esteem for non-university paths. However, as noted in chapter 5, there is growing agreement internationally that a unified curriculum—which provides youth with the foundation for adult and working life while validating rich and deep informal (work-based) learning—is the way forward (cf.

Hager & Hyland, 2003; Hodgson & Spours, 1997; Raffe, Howieson, Spours, & Young, 1998). This chapter concurs that a socially just approach requires less streaming and more integrated programs that value young people's learning strengths, meet them where they are, and allow them to achieve a range of life goals.

High School Streaming

The school creates differences among students by offering them different kinds of knowledge. . . . Different course enrolment sets students on different paths towards the labour market. . . . In a very concrete organizational form, one can see in high school course enrolments the genesis of divisions that shape adult life. (Gaskell, 1992, p. 37)

What Is Streaming?

Davies and Guppy (2014) define streaming (referred to as "tracking" in the US) as the practice of sorting students into different groups: typically, an upper stream bound for post-secondary schooling and lower streams offering vocational training. Streaming takes different forms at different levels of schooling. For example, in elementary school, it is perhaps most evident in the placement of students labelled "behavioural, slow learning, and learning disabled" in special education classes (Curtis, Livingstone, & Smaller, 1992, p. 53); at the secondary level it is evident in the distribution of students across various types and levels of courses. Beyond streaming by course, sorting of students is evident in other features of the organization of schooling—in private schools and school fees, in the differentiation of programming in schools (e.g., French immersion, International Baccalaureate, apprenticeship), and in policies related to school choice and transportation. Fundamentally, streaming is about the degree of stratification of school offerings and access to these offerings.

Internationally, school systems differ in the amount and types of streaming, and the levels or ages at which youth are streamed. For example, countries with a dual education system—such as Germany, Austria, Denmark, and German-speaking Switzerland—stream students early into specialized institutions, which allow for little flexibility or movement (Grubb, 2006). The potential benefit of such specialization is the provision of high-quality vocational education and training programs. In comparison, North American school programs tend to be more open but also less coherent and transparent.

History of Streaming

In Canada, the organization of schooling and streaming has evolved over time. Recall our discussion in chapter 3 about the campaign for technical education in the late 1800s and early 1900s in Ontario. Educational historian Bruce Curtis documents these changes over a broader period. He notes that schools have been used to produce "cheerful obedience and industrial work habits . . . while equipping the population with fundamental skills of literacy," and attributes the situation to the 1850 School Act's centralized control over elementary education (Clanfield et al., 2014, p. 49). Curtis reports that in the 1850s and 1860s the Education Department tried to establish elementary schooling for the mass of population and grammar schooling for the sons of the professional, large-landowning, and capitalist class. The 1871 School Act saw secondary schools offering English and commercial courses, and collegiate schools offering instruction in classics leading to university.

In addition to class bias, the evolving organization of schooling reflected racist beliefs. Grace-Edward Galabuzi writes, "from the beginnings of French and British settlement and the colonization of Canada's First Nations, differential pathways for the children of racialized newcomers and Aboriginal communities have led to poorer educational outcomes and potentially lifelong disadvantages in socio-economic status" (Clanfield et al., p. 188). For example, in different periods segregated schooling was not uncommon for racialized students, as documented in Knight's (2012) article about black students in the mid nineteenth century in Canada's West, and in Stanley's (2012) article about Chinese students in British Columbia in the early part of the twentieth century.

In the mid 1800s, Egerton Ryerson proposed the development of industrial labour schools for Aboriginal children, based on principles of basic education, hard work, and religious devotion (Schissel & Wotherspoon, 2003). The intent of residential school policy was to destroy Indigenous culture and reconstruct "Indian" children as active participants in the industrial economy. Forced schooling of registered Indian children at the end of the nineteenth century provided free child and youth labour for farms, industries, and households, persisting into the middle of twentieth century. Further, inequities in schooling for Aboriginal students were perpetuated by practices of giving them less time in classrooms, less-educated teachers, and inadequate school funding (Barman, 2012).

The racialized segregation of schooling has left a legacy. The denial of Aboriginal identity, removal of children from families, severed links between culture and spirituality, erosion of languages, undermining of traditional leadership, and denial of political rights and the right to self-determination have all contributed to lower educational achievement for Aboriginal students (Aboriginal Learning Knowledge Centre, 2009). It is no surprise then that their enrolment in higher education continues to be lower and shows less growth than non-Aboriginal enrolment since 2002 (Association of Universities and Colleges of Canada, 2011). The 2012 Aboriginal Peoples Survey also showed that 43 percent of off-reserve First Nations people, 26 percent of Inuit, and 47 percent of Métis aged 18 to 44 had PSE credentials, with no significant change from the 2006 survey (Statistics Canada, 2013). The corresponding figure for the non-Aboriginal population in 2011 was 64 percent with PSE credentials, according to the National Household Survey.

As chapter 3 suggests, the question of how different students should be educated, in the campaign of the late 1800s for technical education, has resulted in ongoing debate and a variety of "answers." For example, new vocational schools funded through the Technical and Vocational Training Assistance Act in the 1960s were seen as a solution for dealing with exceptional students (Ellis and Axelrod, forthcoming). The percentage of students participating in special education grew from 3.9 percent in 1960 to 7.2 percent in 1974, and most of this growth was absorbed in opportunity and academic–vocational classes, "which brought together children who had been labeled 'slow learners,' 'limited ability,' or 'educable mentally retarded'—basically the same groups of children with IQs between 50 and 75, or 75 and 90, who had been attending these classes in the 1950s" (Martell [1974], cited in Ellis and Axelrod, forthcoming). Notably, classes for "new Canadians" fell under the board's "special education" umbrella.

The geographical placement of programs is also revealing. Eight new high schools that were opened in Toronto in the 1960s for the lowest levels of streaming (four vocational schools and four special high schools), were located in neighbourhoods south of Bloor Street; school enrolments consisted almost entirely of students from working-class, ethnic/racial minority, and single-parent families (Clanfield et al., 2014). In Ontario during the 1970s, a working-class child ran a 10 times greater chance of ending up in a vocational program than did a child of the professional or managerial class (Curtis, Livingstone, & Smaller, 1992). Students were also segregated by gender; the four vocational schools were single-sex (male), and vocational programs within schools reflect gendered labour-market divisions.

By the 1970s, some students, parents, and teachers were resisting early streaming and stigmatization (Clanfield et al., 2014). For example, in February 1970, nine Toronto women from the inner city—the "Trefann Court mothers"—presented a brief to Toronto Board of Education trustees, alleging that the public schools discriminated against poor and immigrant children by streaming them disproportionately into dead-end special classes (Ellis & Axelrod, forthcoming). A Toronto school board study conducted around this time found that only 15 percent of former students from vocational programs held jobs related to the program in which they had been enrolled, while 40 percent were unemployed (Reich & Zeigler, 1972). Although the Robarts Plan was discarded in 1969, the legacy of several hundred vocational school buildings in Ontario helped ensure the continuation of streaming. As noted in chapter 3, a credit system (with advanced, general, and basic streams) replaced the arts and science, business and commercial, and science, technology, and trades programs.

Contemporary Streaming in Ontario Schools

Harry Smaller suggests that inequitable streaming practices persist in Ontario schooling. He argues that the rhetoric of equally valued pathways for students taking different course streams rings hollow, given the different realities of their destinations (Clanfield et al., 2014). In grades 9 and 10, students are streamed into "applied," "academic," or "locally developed" courses, while in grades 11 and 12, students take "workplace," "college," "college/university" or "university" streams. A mathematics resource guide for teachers distinguishes between "academic" and "applied" courses in grades 9 and 10 as follows:

> *Academic courses* develop students' knowledge and skills through the study of theory and abstract problems. These courses focus on the essential concepts of a subject and explore related concepts as well. They incorporate practical applications as appropriate.

> *Applied courses* focus on the essential concepts of a subject, and develop students' knowledge and skills through practical applications and concrete examples. Familiar situations are used to illustrate ideas, and students are given more opportunities to experience hands-on applications of the concepts and theories they study. (Ministry of Education, 2005, p. 6)

For grades 11 and 12, a mathematics resource guide for teachers distinguishes between "university," "university/college," "college," and "workplace" preparation courses as follows:

University preparation courses are designed to equip students with the knowledge and skills they need to meet the entrance requirements for university programs.

University/college preparation courses are designed to equip students with the knowledge and skills they need to meet the entrance requirements for specific programs offered at universities and colleges.

College preparation courses are designed to equip students with the knowledge and skills they need to meet the requirements for entrance to most college programs or for admission to specific apprenticeship or other training programs.

Workplace preparation courses are designed to equip students with the knowledge and skills they need to meet the expectations of employers, if they plan to enter the workplace directly after graduation, or the requirements for admission to many apprenticeship or other training programs. (Ministry of Education, 2007, p. 8)

But, despite the presentation of courses as distinct but equal in value, Smaller suggests that outcomes for students in different streams differ considerably. For example, Toronto District School Board 2013 fact sheets suggest that graduation rates after five years of secondary schooling were only 42 percent for students taking vocational or "locally developed" courses and 59 percent for students taking "applied" courses—compare this to 88 percent for students taking "academic" courses (cited in Clanfield et al., 2014, p. 97). Province-wide data for Ontario show that, of the students who went directly into an apprenticeship program, 5.1 percent had enrolled in a "locally developed" math course in grade 9, 50.2 percent had enrolled in "applied," and 43.8 percent enrolled in "academic" levels (King et al., 2009). In comparison, 96.9 percent of students who went directly to university took an "academic" grade 9 math course. It appears that, to an extent, students are self-selecting based on their aspirations, although it is noteworthy that a significant proportion of youth apprentices are taking "university stream" courses. Relatedly, our study of former high school apprentices[3] in Ontario and Alberta found that 23 percent aspired to university education, and 20 percent aspired to college education (Taylor, Lehmann, Raykov, & Hamm, 2013). Of those who planned to enroll in formal education in the next five years, almost one-third planned on college while roughly another quarter planned on university. Therefore, youth are clearly resisting the "destination" discourse of policy-makers, which raises the question of whether new streaming will shift the old status hierarchy (discussed in chapter 5), and more importantly, whether it might be beneficial to de-stream entirely.

Statistics demonstrate differences in pathways for different groups. Although more young women than men in Ontario schools in 2006–7 went directly to university (57.7 percent), far fewer young women went directly from secondary school to an apprenticeship (25.3 percent) (King et al., 2009). As well, fewer English-as-a-second-language (ESL) students who started secondary school in 2002–3 completed a secondary school diploma (62.6 percent compared to 75.7 percent for non-ESL students) and enrolled in university (26.3 percent compared to 30.6 percent). Researchers in Alberta have also noted poor schooling outcomes for ESL students (Roessingh, 2004; Watt & Roessingh, 2001). A study in the Toronto District School Board found that the proportion of refugee[4] students enrolled in "advanced" courses was lower than the corresponding proportion of the general population (Yau, 1996). First Nations students enrolled in Ontario public, Catholic, and private secondary schools, and funded by Indian and Northern Affairs Canada in 2005–6, were also less likely than other students to complete a secondary school diploma or to enroll in university (2.8 percent vs. 21.6 percent) or college (8.2 percent vs. 12 percent) (King et al., 2009).

In the Toronto District School Board (TDSB), secondary school graduation rates also vary by ethnicity. For example, of the 25 percent of students who do not graduate, disproportionate numbers are "Aboriginal, Black (African heritage), Hispanic, Portuguese and those of Middle Eastern background" (TDSB, 2010, p. 3).[5] Grace-Edward Galabuzi suggests that racialized streaming occurs not only in terms of course selection but also through the deployment of "youth at risk" (YAR) discourses and interventions, and zero-tolerance school policies (Clanfield et al., 2014). YAR discourse tends to reinforce racial hierarchies by constructing working-class, racialized, and Aboriginal youth as deviant, dangerous, threatening, and risky. The stereotyping experienced by black youth also tends to undermine their educational experience and marginalize them in schools, which understandably has a negative impact on their educational outcomes and life chances. Race also intersects with social class and gender. For example, students in low-income schools in Ontario in 2006 were four times as likely to be immigrants and racialized, and five times as likely to be of Aboriginal identity. Further, in the Toronto District School Board black females from professional backgrounds were the "least likely female group to confirm university acceptance" (Clanfield et al., 2014, p. 238).

Parents' educational attainment and careers continue to influence student outcomes; according to 2013 TDSB fact sheets, 17 percent of youth with high school–educated parents drop out of secondary school, compared to only 8 percent of youth with university-educated parents (Clanfield et al., 2014). Moreover, the same fact sheets show that 35 percent of youth from families in unskilled or clerical work do not apply to a PSE program, compared to 15 percent of youth from professional families (Clanfield et al., 2014). Therefore, although "university for all" should not necessarily be the goal (cf. Rosenbaum, 2001),[6] the fact that socio-demographic factors shape how students populate different streams means that equity implications are important to address.

Youth in Transition Survey Findings about Streaming

Chapter 5 referred briefly to findings from my co-authored, cross-Canada study of streaming in four provinces (Alberta, British Columbia, Ontario, and Saskatchewan), which was based on data from 15-year-olds and their parents who participated in the 2000 Youth in Transition Survey (YITS) (Taylor & Krahn, 2009). Similar to the findings cited above, Harvey Krahn and I found that, overall, fewer students from families with lower income and lower levels of parental education participate in course streams that lead to university (Taylor & Krahn, 2009). For example, in Alberta, 79 percent of students who were taking university-bound course streams in English, math, and science had parents with at least one degree, compared to 52 percent of students whose parents did not have a degree. Similarly, in Ontario, 73 percent of students who were taking university-bound course streams in English, math, and science had family incomes[7] above $90,000 a year, compared to only 49 percent of those with family incomes under $30,000 a year.

However, our analysis showed that the proportion of students whose first language was English or French who were taking secondary school courses that could qualify for university was slightly lower than those whose first language was neither English nor French.[8] Further, we found that "visible minority" students were more likely than others to have open PSE options; however, our inability to disaggregate these data is problematic, since we know that the outcomes of different racialized, "visible minority" groups vary significantly (Dei et al., 1997). For instance, Indigenous student outcomes were not reported separately in YITS data, so we could not make comparisons with this group.

In addition to family background, our study considered the impact of province, school size (often associated with community size), and school type (sectarian including Catholic and private religious schools, and non-sectarian) on streaming outcomes (Taylor & Krahn, 2009). Our multivariate analysis of the determinants of open PSE options found that province of residence had the strongest impact on the chance that a 15-year-old would have all options (including university) open in grade 10; young people living in Saskatchewan were much more likely than their peers in Ontario, British Columbia, and Alberta to have open PSE options. Young people living in Alberta were least likely to have open PSE options amongst the provinces examined (Taylor & Krahn, 2009). This raises important questions about provincial differences in curriculum streams, policies, and practices.

When we controlled for province of residence and other variables, the next strongest effect was associated with parental education. The chance of having all PSE options open was 2.5 times higher for 15-year-olds who had at least one university-educated parent than it was for youth whose parents did not complete university. Family income also had a statistically significant net effect. In addition, young women were more likely than young men to have open PSE options, other things being equal. The same was true of racialized immigrant youth, young people attending sectarian schools, and those enrolled in larger schools. But compared to the effects of family background (i.e. parents' education and income) these effects were not as strong.

Canadian authors (Clanfield et al., 2014; Curtis, Livingstone, & Smaller, 1992; Martell, 2009; Taylor & Krahn, 2009) problematize streaming because of evidence that student outcomes continue to be stratified by social class, race, and gender. D.W. Livingstone argues that there is no social justification for children from upper-middle-class families to be twice as likely to be in the academic stream in secondary school and four times as likely to complete university as working-class children (in Clanfield et al., 2014). The response of schools, which tend to focus either on innate differences between different groups of students or on cultural deficits perpetuated in families, ignore the "enduring structures of political dominance that frame and condition the reproduction of . . . differences in schooling" (Clanfield et al., 2014, p. 30).

For example, vocational-focused programs operate primarily in Toronto's lowest-income neighbourhoods, whereas programs such as French immersion are more likely to be offered in affluent areas (Parekh, Killoran, & Crawford, 2011). More students with university-educated parents were enrolled in schools that did not offer high school apprenticeship programs than in schools that did offer such programs (39.4 percent vs. 29.5 percent). Special,[9] vocational, and basic education schools were almost five times more likely than academically elite schools to have at least one-third of students from low-income households. Therefore, it "appears that a divide has been drawn between programs geared toward students coming from higher and lower income households" (Parekh, Killoran, & Crawford, 2011, p. 273). Despite the discourse of viable pathways for all youth, Smaller adds that few viable alternatives are being provided for those who leave elementary school without the academic skills to cope in the new applied and academic programs (Clanfield et al., 2014).

Drawing on my own research, I agree that schools continue to contribute to social inequality, and that pathways for youth leading directly to work or to apprenticeship are less valued. The policy direction toward standards-based accountability and school choice in Alberta and other provinces has exacerbated this tendency (Taylor, 2001). At the same time, the valuation of programs is related to regional labour markets and associated demand for different kinds of workers. For example, tradespeople in Alberta, particularly those working in oil and gas or related areas, thrive in boom times, in terms of employment and earnings. Therefore, it is clear that regional opportunity structures make a difference (Lehmann, Taylor, & Hamm, 2013). In the sections that follow, I discuss findings from my research, which focused mostly on the experiences of students in high school apprenticeship programs, and on educational pathways for Aboriginal youth.

What Happens to Vocational Programming in an Education Market?

> Our biggest battle, to be honest with you, over about 30 years is the stigma attached to a trade school. (Edmonton school principal cited in Taylor, 2006a, p. 44)

The above statement is from a secondary school principal within the Edmonton Public School Board (EPSB) in Alberta, which became known nationally and internationally for its openness to school choice and alternative programs. My study explored the question of what happens to school programming in a district of choice that is characterized by competition for students and a high degree of student mobility across schools.

Interviews with 17 secondary public school principals led to the following conclusions:

- Principals avoid reputations of schools as "vocational" and seek reputations as "academic" schools;

- School programs continue to reflect their neighbourhood demographics; and
- The programming offered to different groups is valued unequally (Taylor, 2006a).

Principals in at least two Edmonton secondary schools referred to their institutions' history as trade schools. However, open boundaries and declining enrolments put pressure on these schools to reinvent themselves, which is exactly what happened. One traded shops for studios, becoming an arts-focused school in the mid 1980s, while the other switched shops for computer labs, becoming a science and technology–focused school in the early 1990s. Since then, competition for students has increased and principals have become more sensitive to the effects of programming on the composition of the student body. For example:

> *Principal:* We have a lot of students that wish to register for our automotive program as well as our cosmetology program, and those programs are thriving. Well at some point, you have to then ask yourself . . . should we look at expanding the program? Or should we then look to the district offering it in another school? And again, balancing things off. Because we've known from our history that, in the same way you can have students that refer to a school as an IB [International Baccalaureate] school, some schools in the past have had a reputation of being a vocational-directed school.
>
> *Interviewer:* Is that negative?
>
> *Principal:* I believe if the school becomes identified as a vocational school, it will lose its draw for a student who wishes to have a more regular high school experience . . . in the past we've had that, and one of the reasons we've had to look at changing the reputation of a high school was because it got too strong a vocational reputation. (Taylor, 2006a, p. 44)

At the same time, principals did not see a problem with their school being identified as an academic one. In fact, by the time of my study, every high school within the public school board had introduced a university preparation program—either an Advanced Placement (AP) or an IB program, to attract "high flyers" because "they're the school's bread and butter … they give the schools good reputations" (p. 44). Therefore, talk of "balancing school populations" was code for attracting more academic students. However, this balance had not been reached in most schools in the district. For example, low-income neighbourhood schools had higher proportions of students labelled as "ESL and special needs," and fewer enrolled in AP or IB courses, while the reverse was true for schools in higher-income neighbourhoods (Taylor, 2006a). Further, the percentage of grade 10 students enrolled in academic courses ranged from a low of 35 percent in a low-income neighbourhood school to 100 percent in an IB school that admitted students from across the district based on entrance examination scores. Thus, choice does not seem to balance school populations; in fact it may perpetuate more inequity across schools, as other researchers have argued (Ball, 2003).

The question of how students respond to streaming within and across schools is addressed by research on "tracking" in Flemish schools, which found that study involvement (i.e., how concerned students are about going to school and studying) was lower for low-track students in a school with both academic and vocational tracks (a multilateral school) than it was in segregated vocational schools (Van Houtte & Stevens, 2009). The authors conclude that the benefits of contact with a higher-track group were outweighed by the feelings of relative deprivation experienced by lower track students:

> Our research shows that putting different tracks together in one school *while maintaining a firm distinction between tracks* is certainly not a solution and might even provoke the opposite of the desired effect, namely, even more negative school attitudes in lower track students. (p. 965) [emphasis added]

This study suggests that rather than "rearranging deck chairs," which is what school choice essentially does, policy-makers should start to ask more critical questions about streamed curriculum and its effects on different students.

What is offered to students who are not seen as destined for PSE? My study of Edmonton high schools found that, reflecting the lower valuation of "vocational" programming, apprenticeship[10] credits were awarded in only one-third of high schools. Work-experience credits were popular:

> Work experience is supposed to be a program designed by the student in concert with the principal or counselor and that program is then individually tailored to that student with individual results and assessments put in place. That's all supposed to be coordinated by the work experience coordinator or by the principal in a

small school. So quite frankly, it's rare when that happens according to Hoyle. . . . Most times, it's a cheap employee and you get five credits for pumping gas, and that sort of thing. . . . I think in Edmonton Public [School Board] we've cleaned up a lot of that . . . by ensuring that work experience coordinators are very careful about ensuring there's an individual program plan. (School district representative cited in Taylor, 2006a, p. 50)

However, a principal in a low-income neighbourhood comments:

The work experience [course] has a very strong footing in this school but not for the right reason. So many of our kids work to survive and when you figure out you can work and get credit, then you go to work experience. Does it do the training aspect that it's supposed to? I would say "no" and I would say we're not the only school where it would be "no." (p. 51)

Such comments suggest that programs for "work-destined" students may not be providing students with either appropriate workplace skills or the knowledge needed to progress to higher education. In contrast, the principal of a "science magnet school" discusses a program for "high-flying science students" who want to learn about work applications and career opportunities:

The person who's been in charge for the last three years has just done a fantastic job and I really see a niche for the job that he's done. He runs it very much like a work experience program, but instead of working they're out with people in the science and technology fields. So it's like a sort of a job shadowing type of thing, and it works incredibly well. Lots of people from the university, and it's a very, very powerful program for kids. (Taylor, 2006a, p. 52)

Similarly, a principal at the IB school mentioned above speaks with enthusiasm about a program for his students:

Every summer [students] will work in the labs, an awful lot of them are interested in the health sciences field so they will develop contacts with professors over there, either through their biology, physics, or chemistry teachers here who are in touch with them. A lot of the people [at the university] are former graduates of the school so that's a nice contact. . . . They come back to the school occasionally and give special lessons or enrichment classes after school for both staff and students. . . . You can go to the university hospital any day of the week . . . and you'll see our students there volunteering. (p. 52)

The contrast between what secondary schools offer to the "bright lights" compared to what they offer to "twinkies" (as one principal described students seen as less capable) was stark (Taylor, 2006a). Further, students across tracks recognize these differences in learning opportunities and status (Hallam & Ireson, 2007).

The Failure of Schooling for Indigenous Youth

As argued by authors cited above, the relationships between families' low socio-economic status, students' racialized identity, and students' poor educational outcomes have been documented, and the practice of streaming is believed to perpetuate inequalities (Clanfield et al., 2014; Curtis, Livingstone & Smaller, 1992). These observations are reinforced by research that addresses school-to-work transitions for Indigenous youth. For example, our study of Aboriginal youth transitions in northern Alberta's oil sands region suggested that First Nations and Métis communities were not benefitting as much as others from the economic boom (Taylor, Friedel, & Edge, 2009, 2010). Few Aboriginal youth were employed by the large oil and gas corporations in trades or professional occupations, often because they did not have a high school diploma; instead they ended up working in temporary labouring jobs. Our focus was on First Nation communities that were part of the Athabasca Tribal Council (ATC) in this region.

Student results in Northlands School Division, where the First Nations communities were located (and which has the highest proportion of First Nations, Métis and Inuit [FNMI] students in the province) were significantly poorer than for the province overall, in terms of dropout rates and three-year high school completion rates. Many students from ATC communities bused to Fort McMurray or boarded there to attend school at age 15 because there were no high schools in their communities. Between 2005 and 2008, the graduation rates in the two Fort McMurray school districts for FNMI students were just under 60 percent (Taylor, Friedel, & Edge, 2009).[11] Further, the proportion of FNMI high school students in the stream leading to an early school-leaving certificate was double the proportion of FNMI students in the school population (Taylor, Friedel, & Edge, 2009). There are multiple reasons for these outcomes; undeniably, they reflect colonial legacies of institutionalized racism, including the intergenerational trauma resulting from epidemics, displacement from lands, suppression of ceremonies and languages, and loss of children to residential schools and child welfare agencies (Brant Castellano, 2008).

But outcomes are also tied to continuing inequalities between schools on First Nation reserves and provincial schools. For example, our study of First Nation youth involved in a high school health internship program in southern Alberta found schools on reserves were challenged by fewer-than-average resources and higher-than-average proportions of students with special needs (Taylor & Steinhauer, 2010). Students' access to post-secondary education was limited by the scarcity of federal funding for First Nations students and the limited availability of programs near reserves. As we found in northern Alberta, the additional financial and emotional costs of moving away from home and leaving behind peers, family, and culture presented challenges for youth. Finally, although some students wanted to return to work on the reserve after pursuing post-secondary education, opportunities for professional work were very limited.

Further, education policies did not address the youth's priorities. For example, First Nations youth did not strive for a pathway that defined success primarily in terms of university certification and high earnings. Rather, several had taken on family commitments and expressed a strong sense of collective community responsibility. Participants in our study recognized the costs of mainstream success—working parents with less time for their children, loss of culture as youth try to assimilate, and the continuing out-migration from reserves. Clearly, these costs must be acknowledged and addressed in any policies related to Indigenous education generally and school-to-work transitions in particular. The Aboriginal Learning Knowledge Centre recommends that Aboriginal communities, governments, and researchers develop a common, balanced understanding of what constitutes success in Aboriginal learning (2009), arguing that failure to do so results in information that is irrelevant to Aboriginal communities and that fails to inform effective social policy.

The experiences of urban Aboriginal students are both similar to and distinct from the issues faced by students in First Nation communities. Our research at a high school in Edmonton that provides opportunities for early school-leavers to earn a high school diploma as an alternative to life on the street (Wishart, Taylor & Shultz, 2006) confirmed that "bottom streaming" often leads to poor and racialized students "physically dropping out of school or psychically dropping out of the bottom stream programs in which they are placed" (Martell, 2009). The majority of these students lived independently or in group homes, and most lived in poverty; over half identified as Aboriginal, compared to around 6 percent for Edmonton overall. Most came to this school after negative early schooling experiences, according to a teacher:

> They're usually put in programs or courses [in public schools] intended for behavior problems because they're not able to meet the standards for school and as a result they act out, they've poor attendance, and it's just a recipe for disaster. (Cited in Wishart, Taylor, & Shultz, 2006, p. 301)

This study of urban youth confirmed that "youth at risk" discourse can be double edged—although it opens doors to intervention, labelling can perpetuate stigma while ignoring systemic problems (see also Clanfield et al., 2014; Wotherspoon & Schissel, 2001). My co-authors and I argue that socially just responses are constrained by education policies that work at cross-purposes and by "deficit thinking" about these youth and their families, which constructs them as lacking and blames them for their problems:

> In particular, market approaches that encourage the differentiation of schools, programs, and course streams, and the funding and identification of students with special needs appear to vertically sort students in a way that produces as well as responds to youth at risk. (Wishart, Taylor, & Shultz, 2006, p. 293)

For example, teachers at this school felt pressured to engage in labelling students in order to qualify for the funding needed to help them redress previous educational failures. However, the practice of coding students ran counter to their goals:

> We're constantly struggling with this language—well it's more than a language problem. . . . I tend to see the language of these [program plans for students with special needs] as sort of referring to the student as almost an "it." And I think that we've tried hard to treat them as an "I," somebody who's to be valued. (Teacher cited in Wishart, Taylor, & Shultz, 2006, p. 299)

The negative effects of labelling on students were acknowledged in consultations leading to a report that addressed barriers to high school completion in Alberta:

> One participant expressed dissatisfaction with counseling and the perception of labeling and streaming for lower achieving students.

. . . An Aboriginal participant stated that psychological assessment tools need to be changed, as they are not geared toward Native culture. Another participant stated that high school kids have started to leave "in their heads" as far back as elementary school because of labeling. (Alberta Learning, 2001, p. 17)

In this report, authors link enrolment in "bottom streams" with early school-leaving and lengthier high school completion times (Alberta Learning, 2001, p. 6). But interestingly, instead of challenging streaming, the report recommended making schools more relevant by providing more outreach and vocational programming with links to the workplace. The research cited above points to the complexity of problems related to streaming and Aboriginal youth. However, I would argue that the "solution" of providing more vocational school programming for these youth does not address systemic problems that impact which students have access to "high-status" knowledge. Rather, more attention should be given to developing learning opportunities that combine experiential and theoretical aspects. My studies of high school apprentices provide some useful insights.

The Process and Outcomes of High School Apprenticeship

Our study[12] of the pathways of high school apprentices in Alberta and Ontario confirms that their outcomes depend on *antecedent* factors (e.g., youths' agency, educational experiences, and prior work experiences); *context* factors (including support networks and labour-market conditions); *incidental* factors (e.g., health concerns, business closure); and *process* factors (including the quality of training on and off the job, relationships with trainers, workplace conditions, climate/culture) (Harris & Simons, 2005[13]). As noted in chapter 5, Fuller and Unwin's *expansive–restrictive* continuum is helpful for further analyzing process factors. Recall that expansive learning opportunities in the workplace are characterized by apprentices' exposure to learning experiences across the organization, access to a range of qualifications and qualified mentors, time off for reflection and theoretical instruction, and mentorship in learners' transitions from outsider to expert participant.

Although some of the factors mentioned above are beyond the control of policy-makers and educators, if the objective is a high-quality school-to-work pathway, then they must share responsibility for ensuring that there is open access to programs for all students, that groups who are underrepresented in trades occupations are well supported to achieve success, that work-based education is well integrated with academic studies, and that work-based education is of high quality. Our study of the pathways of high school apprentices who participated in Alberta's Registered Apprenticeship Program (RAP) or Ontario's Youth Apprenticeship Program (OYAP)[14] found that, although many youth spoke highly of their experiences, access to programs was limited, students from underrepresented groups faced particular challenges, work-based education was not integrated with the rest of their school program, and the quality of work-based education was variable.

Currently, youth in high school apprenticeship programs represent a very small proportion of the high school population (under 10 percent). A 2013 survey of Canadian youth aged 13 to 17 found that, despite an increase in the numbers of youth considering careers in the skilled trades since 2004, 53 percent of respondents still identified a university degree as their first-choice post-secondary option. A college diploma was preferred by a quarter of students, whereas an apprenticeship program was the first choice of less than 20 percent of students (Canadian Apprenticeship Forum, 2013).

However, many youth who participated in high school apprenticeships in Alberta or Ontario were very positive about these programs. Those who were most positive usually had completed or were on track to successfully complete their apprenticeship, and their success was related to their comfort with trades work and culture, their ability to find "expansive" training and stable employment, and their families' support. Several had career aspirations that involved further learning, such as gaining certification in another trade, owning their own business, or teaching trades training at a college or high school.

Our 2009 online survey, completed by 173 former high school apprentices (105 in Alberta and 68 in Ontario), found that the majority came from lower than average socio-economic status families (Taylor, Lehmann, Raykov, & Hamm, 2013). The most common occupation for mothers was clerical, sales, or service work, while the most common occupation for fathers (one-third) was skilled trades. Approximately three-quarters of survey respondents indicated that family had played a very important role in their decisions to enter apprenticeship in high school. Interviews with 111 former high school apprentices conducted between 2009 and 2011 (56 from Alberta and 55 from Ontario) also confirm that youth from working-class backgrounds found high school apprenticeships to be a comfortable choice.

In addition to an under representation of youth with university-educated parents, few young women pursued trades work. As noted above, a 2006–7 Ontario study found that only about one-quarter of

Ontario students who went directly from secondary school to an apprenticeship were female (King et al., 2009). Our online survey also found that 74 percent of former high school apprentices were male. Of these, the majority (88 percent) were white, 4 percent were Aboriginal, and almost 11 percent identified as having a disability (most often a learning disability) (Taylor et al., 2013).

Youth from underrepresented groups faced particular challenges in their apprenticeship training. For example, our survey found that fewer females continued to work in their trade after high school (55 percent vs. 79 percent of males), and more females than males discontinued their apprenticeship training (34 percent vs. 25 percent). Earnings of young women in the trades also differed noticeably, with 57 percent of females earning a salary of less than $30,000, compared with 27 percent of males. This is no doubt related to the concentration of females in trades such as hairstyling; valuation of skills continues to be very gendered (Haasler & Gottschall, 2015). Alberta statistics also indicate that the median income for a certified female tradesperson across trades in the Alberta in 2004–5 was $29,371 compared to $52,305 for males (Scullen, 2008).

Our interviews with young women in male-dominated trades revealed that those who were successful in completing training and who continued to work in their trade shared several traits: strong family support, positive workplace mentorship and training, and skills that were in demand (Taylor, Raykov, and Hamm, 2015). For example, Jan[15] was a 22-year-old Red Seal heavy equipment technician working in a small town in Alberta whose income was reported to be between $70,000 and $80,000 a year (Taylor, Raykov, & Hamm, 2015). She noted that a few of her mentors were "phenomenal teachers" who made an effort to ensure that apprentices understood what they were learning. In addition to learning by observing more experienced journeypersons, her company gave her time off work to participate in a provincial trade skills competition, where she was able to demonstrate her skills and extend her networks.

In contrast, those who left their trade were more likely to speak about discriminatory behaviour at work involving bosses, co-workers, and customers. It was clear that women who left, or who were thinking of leaving, were responding to the masculine work culture, not to the work, per se. Our study also found that young women in hairstyling (one of few female-dominated trades) raised different concerns relating to unsatisfactory hours, pay, and job security. The gendered aspects of education, training, and work were also evident when we compared young men in apprenticeship with young women in a high school health-care aide program for Alberta students (Taylor, Servage, & Hamm, 2014). Students saw gendered choices as natural because of early experiences with family members, extended kin networks, and peers. However, their training experiences were quite different; overall, male apprentices had more control over their learning, had more opportunities to learn important skills on the job, and saw more opportunities for vertical and horizontal mobility. There were also evident differences in wages and occupational status, reflecting the power of male trades workers vis-à-vis female workers in lower tiers of health-care work. Further, none of the program partners (schools, intermediary bodies, and employers) took responsibility for encouraging and supporting "non-traditional" training decisions. We conclude that more effort is needed to disrupt gendered vocational streaming by encouraging and supporting women and other "non-traditional" entrants to trades.

In addition to the challenges faced by non-traditional entrants, work-based education was not well integrated with the rest of students' secondary school program. Work-based apprenticeship training was usually an add-on to the high school experience, with little coordination of in-school and out-of-school learning. Although dual credit has potential to integrate apprenticeship training more, the training accessed by most of our apprentices consisted of hours on the job as opposed to in-class training delivered by college or other training providers. Further, the lack of articulation between apprenticeship training and other post-secondary education—particularly university programs—made it difficult for capable youth to move from trades to professional occupations (e.g., engineering). Instead, they were forced to make choices early—choices that reflect broader societal values about different kinds of work. For example, an automotive technician comments:

> I mean, that is the general consensus, that unless you go to university or college you are a failure. . . . You're viewed as . . . you know . . . not as smart as others . . . a person that people will look down upon because education is obviously key, it's a status symbol. (Cited in Lehmann, Taylor, & Wright, 2014, p. 7)

It is therefore not surprising that youth continue to aspire to university streams and destinations, unless they see no other choice.

The employer-driven nature of apprenticeship training also meant that the quality of work-based training was highly variable. Almost half (45 percent) of RAP/OYAP participants had completed their training at the time of our data collection (Taylor et al., 2013). An additional 27 percent were still training and 29 percent had not completed training. Analysis of interview data from 25 high school apprentices in Alberta and Ontario who did not continue training found that several experienced restrictive training in the workplace, including being assigned routine low-level tasks, employers failing to sign off on apprenticeship hours, employers failing to provide release time for in-class schooling, lack of mentorship, and inequities in the allocation of work by supervisors (Taylor, Lehmann, & Raykov, 2014). A former automotive apprentice who left the trade without completing his training felt that government and other partners should pay more attention to making it "easy to be a tradesperson," not just "easy to get into the trades." This would require more regulation and monitoring of work-based training as well as better communication among partners (teachers, trainers, employers, unions, and government).

Overall, our analysis of youth apprenticeship suggests that policy-makers and partners could do more to increase students' knowledge about trades occupations, raise students' awareness of multiple trajectories and skills transfer, make apprenticeship training more expansive, and increase the flexibility of pathways by providing greater articulation between different PSE pathways and opportunities to change direction. Further, my discussion early in this chapter suggests that exploring how to de-stream curriculum is likely to be more valuable than trying to better sort and select students.

Concluding Comments

[T]he assumption that low achievers who invariably, though not always, come from lower social classes, are in some way more motivated by education that is closely linked to their future employability is a legacy of history and product of ideology. (Guile & Young, 2003)

The preceding discussion of streaming in Canadian schools, based on my own and others' research, highlights the material consequences of dividing students into groups based on perceived ability and destinations. As currently conceived, much vocational education and training within secondary schools is geared toward students not destined for university studies and is poorly integrated with academic curriculum. Partly because of reliance on training by employers off campus without sufficient regulation, vocational programs are of uneven quality and often fail to provide clear labour-market benefits. Compared to university degrees, the labour-market returns on student investments in technical diplomas and apprenticeships have been generally lower in Canada (Boothby & Drewes, 2006). Given this evidence, the overrepresentation of working-class and some groups of racialized youth in lower streams implicates streaming in the reproduction of unequal outcomes. But the question remains: What is to be done?

Different writers have noted that educational policy reform has focused more often on re-tooling vocational education than on programming for university-bound students (e.g., Grubb, 2006; Young, 1998). Returning to my argument in chapter 5, rather than continuing to rethink vocational education, perhaps it is time to turn to the kind of connective theoretical vocational curriculum that will address twenty-first-century learning needs. As noted at the beginning of this chapter, writers in the UK and Europe are advocating for a unified curriculum to redress the problems of academic–vocational separation. Paul Hager and Terry Hyland (2003) build on the ideas of John Dewey in advocating for "rich and deep" vocational education, which stresses the full intellectual and social meaning of a vocation, prepares youth for lifelong learning, and is underpinned by social, moral, and aesthetic values—in particular, communitarian and public service values. Similarly, in discussing the way forward for Aboriginal education in Canada, writers advocate for a view of learning as a social process that serves to nurture relationships in the family and throughout the community (Aboriginal Learning Knowledge Centre, 2009).

In parallel, US authors Rosenstock and Steinberg (1999) argue that community projects provide an excellent way of integrating vocational and academic knowledge; they suggest that such projects encourage creativity in students by bringing the humanities to vocational education and vice versa. Their discussion of the democratic culture of the program at Rindge School of Technical Arts in Massachusetts echoes some of the recommendations of Ontario writers for de-streamed schools (Clanfield et al., 2014). These recommendations include cooperative management by educators, parents, learners, and other community members in schools; more dialogical and project-oriented teaching; and more opportunity for students to broaden their sense of community and build their capacity to participate.

My recent experience as director of Community Service–Learning at a Canadian university suggests that this kind of experiential learning, integrated into curriculum, could usefully inform discussions about the future of vocational education and training. In particular, community-based projects have the potential to expose youth to real world problems and solutions, create networks of learning that extend beyond schools, and break down the divisions between theory and practice, school and workplace, that have been so unproductive. This direction will be discussed further in chapter 7.

Concluding Thoughts

Youth today may be forgiven for thinking the transitions they are facing are like a game of snakes and ladders—they move forward only to slide back again. Teachers, parents, and policy-makers tell them that they must pursue education beyond high school, assess and respond to labour-market trends, be flexible and adaptable, and keep upgrading their skills as they inch their way into the adult world. But at the same time, good jobs—jobs that develop, utilize, and reward their skills—are hard to find (Livingstone, 2010). This chapter's discussion about rethinking vocational education in secondary schools is informed by this reality. I have argued that a rich and deep vocational education that also acknowledges the cultural and social purposes of education is required.

Previous chapters examined secondary school education policy aimed at connecting school and work, both in the past and in the present. Although both the average educational attainment and the range of possible career pathways for youth have increased, the way we value, measure, and reward different kinds of knowledge in schools (and in society) continues to place limits on some students. Divisions between academic and vocational, and formal and informal learning are especially problematic. Traditional approaches to vocational education that limit students must be disrupted. In chapter 4 I used the word *vocational* to describe educational functions and processes that aim to prepare and equip individuals and groups for working life (Skillbeck, Connell, Lowe, & Tait, 1994). Such preparation is not narrow—instead it aims to develop concepts, ideas, and skills that are generalizable, are capable of application in varied and changing circumstances, and can be built upon, developed, and extended (Skillbeck, Connell, Lowe, & Tait, 1994).

My conclusion here considers these questions: What is the purpose of vocational education and how has it changed with changes in work? What are the implications of changes in purpose for secondary school curriculum? How should work-based learning be organized? How can students be better supported in vocational learning activities? My responses to these questions involve reflection on how they have been answered in the past and how they might be addressed in the future.

The Shifting Purposes of Vocational Education

The purpose of vocational education has shifted over time. As noted in chapter 2, the establishment of industrial schools in the late 1800s was motivated by an interest in providing moral education to marginalized youth, while preparing them to learn the work norms and rules of the factory (Morrison, 1974). Today, vocational education is seen as a way to direct students into a range of education and training pathways with the objective of developing transferable knowledge and skills.

Aims and approaches also vary across nations. As noted in chapter 4, Nordic countries with strong traditions of social democracy tend to have wider, societal goals for education (Gleeson & Keep, 2004). Sweden, for example, has been cited as an example of a country with an integrated general and vocational education system. In countries with strong VET systems, such as Germany, vocational and general education tend to be more separate, but the former is valued; work experience contributes to the development of occupational competence and occupational identity. Meanwhile, in countries with strong general education systems, such as Canada, work experience is aimed at teaching students to be independent adults and assisting them in their transition to the labour market (Guile & Griffiths, 2001). However, vocational education programs in Canada struggle to attract students because of their low status.

Traditional approaches to vocational education assume a functionalist view of education and work; students are expected to adapt to and be assimilated into a work environment that is stable and transparent. But work environments are often not stable or transparent, and a key premise of "knowledge economy" discourse is that workers need to do more than "fit" into workplaces. For example, Alberta Education's (2010) Inspiring Education Steering Committee report states:

> In the future, Alberta's economy will be even more knowledge-based, diverse, and grounded in value-added industries. As never before, the next generation will need to be innovative, creative, and skilled in managing knowledge as a resource.

Accordingly, new vocationalism—which advocates for a more inclusive general workforce preparation, with more integration of academic and vocational learning—has gained appeal. However, chapter 4 argued that the implementation of new vocationalism has been less successful than expected. Education systems have emphasized pedagogic approaches that support the study and assessment of subjects in isolation from one another; furthermore, these subjects are separated from practical contexts. For example, our research indicates that high school apprenticeship programs operate separately from the rest of students' programs.

Envisioning the Transformation of Education

Recent visioning documents in K–12 education in Alberta and British Columbia call for transformative changes in education, and thus warrant consideration in terms of their implications for vocational education. As noted above, Alberta Education produced a report in 2010 called *Inspiring Education*, which is intended to chart a new course away from the old industrial schooling model toward a more learner-centred and competency-based system. It replaces the 3 R's (reading, [w]riting, [a]rithmetic) with the 3 E's of education for the 21st century: the educated Albertan of 2030 will be an *engaged* thinker and an *ethical* citizen, and will have an *entrepreneurial* spirit. If this vision is realized, curricula will be relevant and accessible in person or virtually, pursued collaboratively or independently, and completed at one's own pace; it will also allow for more interdisciplinary learning. Instead of the dissemination of information and recall of facts, learning will focus on inquiry and discovery. Learners will be encouraged to pursue their passions, make successful transitions to adulthood, and become lifelong learners who contribute to healthy, inclusive communities and thriving economies. The community will play the role of partner in education and there will be more emphasis on experiential learning.

Like "Inspiring Education," BC's "Education Plan" asserts that education is out-dated:

> Our education system is based on a model of learning from another century. To change that, we need to put students at the centre of their own education. We need to make a better link between what kids learn at school and what they experience and learn in their everyday lives. (BC Ministry of Education, 2011)

If the BC vision is realized, students there will also have more freedom to pursue their interests and passions. While building basic skills will continue to be important, there will be more emphasis on key competencies such as critical thinking and problem solving, collaboration and leadership, communication and digital literacy. And while progress will continue to be monitored through "rigorous province-wide assessments" (BC Ministry of Education, 2011, p. 4), educators will have more freedom to decide how and when students are assessed. There will also be greater flexibility in how, when, and where learning takes place. For example, there will be more opportunities for "hands-on learning such as skills, trades and technical training" (BC Ministry of Education, 2015, p. 8). The ministries of Education and Advanced Education jointly created the new position of Superintendent of Graduation and Student Transitions in 2014 to increase the number of students moving from secondary school to PSE programs. Reportedly, work is underway to double apprenticeship and dual-training opportunities for high school students in the next few years (BC Ministry of Education, 2015, p. 12).

While these documents are simply policy rhetoric at this time, it will be interesting to watch how plans unfold. Both sets of recommendations emphasize the use of inquiry-based models and problem-based education in contrast to current pedagogical approaches, which focus more on dissemination of information and recall of facts. A key aim is to relate learning to practical applications. The BC plan calls for provincial curriculum redesign to highlight "key concepts, deeper knowledge, and more meaningful understanding of subject matter"; it will emphasize the "core competencies and skills that students need to succeed in the 21st century" (BC Ministry of Education, 2015, p. 9). Critically, proposed changes encompass both curriculum and pedagogy.

In my view, the transformational nature of new directions will depend partly on the extent to which tensions with the old system can be effectively resolved. For example, how does "rigorous province-wide assessment" fit with more "flexible assessment"? How does the demand for "deep knowledge" fit with discourse of building "competencies"? In addition, what support is there for teachers to undertake their new roles as "architects of learning" rather than "knowledge authorities" (Alberta Education, 2010, p. 7)? And if teachers are no longer "knowledge authorities," who will help students learn specialized knowledge? Finally, will the proposed reforms dismantle or reinforce divisions between different types of knowledge and between groups of students?

Critiques of similar educational reform directions in the UK are instructive. For example, Michael Young (2010) describes reforms there as follows:

The major priorities of the 2008 reforms were to shift the balance away from subject content to topical themes that cut across a range of subjects, and to seek ways of personalising the curriculum by relating it more directly to pupil's everyday knowledge and experiences (p. 23).

Young is concerned about such reforms because, in his view, curriculum subjects play an important role in intellectual development by providing bridges for learners to move from their "everyday concepts" to their associated "theoretical concepts." Teachers then play an important role in drawing on pupils' everyday knowledge in helping them to engage with curriculum concepts to see their relevance. Privileging everyday knowledge runs the risk of separating knowledge from the system of meaning in which it is embedded (cf. Wheelahan, 2012).

A more effective approach to reducing inequality through schooling may be to de-stream or unify academic and vocational (theoretical and practical) curricula rather than to move in the direction of a more "motivational" curriculum" (Raffe et al., 1998; Young, 2010). As suggested in chapter 6, students are currently streamed into different courses located within a status hierarchy that leads to different destinations. It is difficult for them to shift between streams and vocational paths, given the lack of articulation both across course streams and between post-secondary education programs. Further, certain groups of students continue to be overrepresented in low-stream vocational pathways. Whether or not new directions will make a difference for these youth is an important question.

Relating Theory and Practice and the Future of Vocational Education

Q: So are there two types of people in the world? [theoretical and practical]
. . . My roommate . . . If something's broken, he calls me. . . . I am the other way. . . . I do think that there is two sides of it, . . . handy at home, but not on paper. . .

Q: Do you think we can bring those two together?
I'm sure trying. . . . Once you've got the hands on . . . I think it kind of tapers off . . . On the other learning side, I don't think you ever stop. (Former high school apprentice millwright, Alberta)

Young's critique brings us back to my discussion in chapter 5 about how to address historical divisions between academic and vocational learning, theory and practice. A number of writers suggest that a "connective" approach aimed at helping students to relate vertical and horizontal learning is the way forward (Beach, 1999; Guile & Griffiths, 2001). As described in chapter 1, "vertical" knowledge structures transcend specific contexts while "horizontal" knowledge structures are rooted in local, everyday knowledge cultures that are highly context dependent and limited in transferability (Moore, 2009). Encouraging students to relate their vertical and horizontal development calls for connectivity at the level of the education system in terms of opportunities for all youth to move between knowledge and institutional boundaries. Alberta and BC plans for education emphasize the need for schools to be more connected to communities, but how opportunities will be structured and integrated with curriculum is a key question.

While traditional approaches to vocational education assume a simple transfer of knowledge from school to work, a connective model sees students move back and forth between the codified knowledge of curriculum and the situated knowledge of the workplace (Guile & Young, 2003). Typically, it has been left to students to make these connections, as our research on high school apprenticeship suggests. In addition, codified knowledge has often been neglected in favour of situated or experiential knowledge in vocational education—consequently, students may not have access to knowledge that could be valuable and applicable. For example, recall the apprentice's comment quoted in chapter 5, "just [because I'm] interested in auto mechanics doesn't mean I'm incapable of reading." Another apprentice, who lamented his laborious journey from apprenticeship to college to university because of lack of program articulation, suggests:

> I think the counsellors should have made it a lot clearer that by taking the OYAP [Ontario Youth Apprenticeship] program, you're basically cutting off any other potential if you wanted to change your career into more of an academic thing. (Ontario tool-making apprentice)

In contrast, a "connective" approach does not privilege either codified or situated knowledge, instead aiming to help students become "boundary crossers" between schools and work (or community). Boundary-crossing involves students gaining an understanding of how codified knowledge is constructed while learning how to interpret new situations outside of schools in light of this knowledge (Guile & Young, 2003).

Students are encouraged to become critical thinkers, as they test existing knowledge against experience and learn more about the organizational contexts of the workplace and school. This approach echoes Dewey's idea that education and learning are processes of growth characterized by active experimentation and reflective thought. Work experience, from this perspective, involves not only learning particular job tasks but also learning how different workplaces are organized, what the work processes are, what social relations exist in the workplace, and what role is played by unions (Watts, 1991). Further, it includes both local knowledge of particular employers and how they function as well as broader knowledge of work organization and the economy. Thus, youth engage in critical explorations of labour relations and workplace practices rather than simply performing an adaptive role (Shilling, 1987). The connective approach aligns well with a critical pedagogy of work experience, whereby students are provided with the knowledge, skills, and abilities needed to both understand and participate in the political dynamics of the changing workplace (Kincheloe, 1999; Simon et al., 1991). The assumption is that youth can learn to effectively participate in determining the practices that define their working lives.

This model differs markedly from the focus on assimilation and adaptation of students in traditional approaches to vocational education. In a more critical connective model, the role of teachers is to help students use their formal learning to interrogate workplace practices and vice versa (Guile & Griffiths, 2001). At the same time, work-experience providers play a key role in helping students engage in new ways of learning. Both educators and employers (or other community partners) help students learn to contribute to the development of new forms of social practice and the production of new forms of knowledge (Guile & Griffiths, 2001). Clearly, strong reciprocal partnerships between schools, employers, and other players are required for such a vision to be realized. However, the coordinating mechanisms required to develop these kinds of partnerships have been lacking (Taylor, 2009).

A connective model of vocational education sees transitions between school and work as consequential for youth because they involve changes in identity as well as changes in knowledge and skills (Beach, 1999). For example, a young man who reported having poor high school grades discusses his experience being the youngest journeyperson in the RAP program:

> I've grown up, just because I'm so young and being in the trade.
> . . . Knowledge base, I don't try to talk if I don't know anything about it, so I ask. The biggest thing is not being afraid to ask questions. I ask questions all the time. The first thing that pops into my

mind, I'll ask. That's kind of what's got me to the point where I'm at, is just asking questions.

A female tradesperson suggests that she has both grown *in* and grown *into* her job. She recalls feeling a lot of trepidation when she began her training:

Q: *So in your first term you weren't sure if you'd stay with the trade?*
No. . . . I used to be so anxious. When I'd go to work I sometimes had anxiety during the day. I was just like, oh my gosh, because I wasn't completely sure of my surroundings. . . .

But as a certified instrument technician she now mentors others (including another young female apprentice):

I'm a perfectionist and I want [my apprentice] to look up to me as I look up to other people. I tell her every day, if you have any questions just ask me. But I don't know if I'm doing enough. Always at the end of the day I'm like, oh my gosh, I wonder if she really understood that. I want her to think of me as a good teacher and I'm just not sure how to be a good teacher yet.

Both youth have learned to become tradespeople and are clearly interested in continuing development of knowledge and skills.

While many youth in such high school vocational programs succeed in completing their training in a timely way (Taylor, Lehmann, & Raykov, 2014), schools appear to play little role in helping such students to reconstruct their knowledge, skills, and identity in ways that contribute to the creation and metamorphosis of social activity (Beach, 1999). Schools do not act as change agents in partnership with employers and community. Yet arguably this kind of engagement is exactly what is needed if we accept that a knowledge economy requires more creativity and superior problem-solving abilities (as we are constantly reminded). Young apprentices, such as this automotive technician, confirm that students would probably benefit from a more forward-looking approach:

Eventually, what I personally think, is there's not going to be automotive mechanics, there's going to be computer technicians. The push for making hybrid vehicles, I mean, if you ask mechanics what to do on a hybrid vehicle—and I've seen this firsthand—no one really knows. . . . The whole market is completely changing and I personally think in the future it's not going to be the way it is now.

What is being proposed here as "critical connective" learning departs from traditional approaches to vocational education insofar as it encourages learners to question existing knowledge and try out new processes (Guile & Young, 2003). Therefore, the question of how employers and other community partners can become "true partners" (Alberta Education, 2010) is very important. As Beach (1999) notes:

> There is much we have yet to figure out about how schools can support students in becoming someone or something new, negotiating the boundaries of multiple and sometimes contradictory activities, and changing their participation in these activities as the activities themselves change. (p. 31)

In sum, vocational education today is not what it was 100 years ago. It seems obvious that industrial models are no longer appropriate. However, a surviving part of the industrial model has involved the separation of academic and vocational knowledge and the streaming of students into pathways based on this separation. This "survival" needs to be addressed in any educational reforms. Many writers, myself included, believe that the way forward requires us to engage in critical connective approaches to education for all students—approaches that do not subordinate codified curricular knowledge to experiential knowledge or vice versa, but instead explore the linkages and possibilities as students cross the boundaries between school and work. Those involved in such boundary-crossing—teachers, school administrators, employers, and community organizations more broadly—all have important roles to play in encouraging students to learn "about" and "through," rather than simply "for" work.

Notes

Chapter 1

1. Pierre Bourdieu extends Karl Marx's economic notion of capital to include social, cultural, and symbolic capital. For Bourdieu, an individual's economic and cultural capitals determine his or her position in relation to other social actors within social space; by virtue of having certain capitals, a subject is placed within a field of differential power relations. Further, this "objective" social position becomes reflected in one's "subjective" identity. An individual's location in social space is associated with a particular *habitus*—an internalized system of the "production," "perception and appreciation of practices" (Bourdieu 1989:19)—which not only frames an individual's practices and preferences but also provides the "code" by which he or she identifies the social positions of other actors.
2. In the US, President Obama's proposal to provide students with two years of free community college tuition is part of the same discourse of ensuring "young people are getting the skills they need to succeed in the twenty-first century economy" (Simon, 2015).
3. Traditional education aims to transmit to the next generation those skills, facts, and standards of moral and social conduct that adults consider to be necessary for their material and social success. It has been contrasted with progressive educational ideas promoted by writers like John Dewey.

Chapter 2

1. This is a variation of the phrase "The economy, stupid," which was coined by a campaign strategist in Bill Clinton's successful 1992 presidential campaign.
2. In the United States, a 401(k) plan is the tax-qualified, defined contribution pension account defined in subsection 401(k) of the Internal Revenue Code. Under the plan, retirement savings contributions are provided (and sometimes proportionately matched) by an employer, deducted from the employee's pay cheque before taxation.
3. This blog was written in response to an article about why Generation Y's are unhappy: http://iambeggingmymothernottoreadthisblog.com/2013/09/18/im-a-millenial-please-stop-being-a-douche-to-me/
4. Downward harmonization of labour laws and policies usually means adopting practices of nations with the least regulation.
5. Of course, this was before the price of oil slipped below $50 a barrel in early 2015.
6. Berrett and Hoover (2015) note that the UCLA Freshman survey for 2014 (which polls more than 150,000 incoming freshman at 227 four-year colleges and universities in the US) also found that depression among students is on the rise; the share of freshmen (10 percent) who reported "frequently" feeling depressed in the past year is more than three percentage points higher than it was five years ago and is also higher than in the general population (5 percent).

Chapter 3

1. See Ontario Ministry of Education technological education curriculum document for grades 11 and 12: http://www.edu.gov.on.ca/eng/curriculum/secondary/2009teched1112curr.pdf.
2. Discussion of the development of vocational education in Ontario is adapted from Taylor (1997).
3. Agriculture was a field where federal and provincial government shared constitutional responsibility and Canada was still primarily an agricultural nation.
4. This discussion is adapted from Taylor and Lehmann (2002).

Chapter 4

1. The NEET rate in Canada was 13.5 percent in 2010 (up from 11.7 percent in 2008).
2. The youth unemployment rate in OECD countries was estimated at 16.2 percent in the second quarter of 2012, while the rate in Canada was 14.4 percent (ILO, 2013, pp. 85). Rates in Greece and Spain were much higher than in Canada, while the rates in Austria, Germany, Japan, the Netherlands, Norway, and Switzerland were lower (ILO, 2013, pp. 10–11). The NEET rate among 15- to 19-year-olds in Canada was similar to the OECD average in 2010, while the rate for 20- to 24-year-olds was slightly lower (Galarneau, Morisette, and Usalcas, 2013).
3. "K-to-14" refers to education from kindergarten to the first two years of college education. With growing concern about the labour market opportunities for youth who only have a high school diploma, K-to-14 education has become a policy focus.
4. See information about the Provincial Partnership Council at http://www.ontario employer.ca/.
5. At the time of writing, the OBEP was evolving into a "nationally recognized system integrator," the Canadian Business Education Partnership (CBEP). See http://obep.on.ca/about-us.html.
6. Career academies were first developed in the US in the 1980s with the aim of restructuring large high schools into small learning communities and creating better pathways from high school to further education and the workplace.
7. Information about dual credit was found at http://education.alberta.ca/department/ipr/dualcredit.aspx.

Chapter 5

1. Unless otherwise indicated, the apprentices cited in this section were part of my research study with Wolfgang Lehmann tracking high school apprentices in Ontario and Alberta a few years after high school. Interviews were conducted with 111 former high school apprentices between 2009 and 2011.
2. The resulting 1917 Smith-Hughes Act specified particular vocational programs, created administrative procedures, and prescribed skills-based training programs for instruction in agriculture, trade and industries, and home economics. It therefore established a precedent of federal–state financing for vocational education within a unitary administrative school structure.
3. See, for example, Taylor and Watt-Malcolm (2007), Taylor, Lehmann, and Raykov (2014), Lehmann, Taylor, and Hamm (2013), and Taylor and Freeman (2011).

4. Apprentices can challenge their exam if they have sufficient on-the-job hours without attending the classroom training. Usually in-class training is done through block release (usually four weeks) from their workplace to attend trade-specific training in a college classroom.
5. Applied academics was a stream of courses introduced in British Columbia in 1994 that was intended to link abstract classroom knowledge with more concrete workplace application (Gaskell, Nicol, and Tsai, 2004).

Chapter 6

1. The war and mass production affected the fortunes of this small custom-furniture business and, like many contemporary immigrants coming to Canada with hopes for a better life, my father ended up working in a series of semi-skilled jobs unrelated to his trade.
2. In contrast, countries like Germany integrate vocational education more effectively into the school system; apprenticeships include a much wider range of occupations and are seen as a viable career pathway (see for example, Heinz and Taylor, 2005).
3. Our study included survey responses from 173 youth, five years or more after their enrolment in a high school apprenticeship program in Ontario (68) and Alberta (105).
4. Refugee students struggle to be successful in secondary school because they and/or their families are often challenged by physical and mental health concerns, limited labour market skills, and low levels of formal education (Sadler and Clark, 2014).
5. In 2001, nearly one half (47 percent) of the black population, about 310 500, lived in the Toronto census metropolitan area (CMA) (Milan and Tran, 2004).
6. James Rosenbaum wrote a book in 2001 called *Beyond College for All: Career Paths for the Forgotten Half*, in which he analyzed what was happening for "non-college bound" youth in the US compared to other countries, and advocated for more effective programs to address their needs.
7. Family income information came from interviews with parents in the Youth in Transition Survey.
8. YITS data asked about students' first language, while the King et al. (2009) study reported students who had taken an ESL course in secondary school. This raises questions about the age at which students must learn English or French, and the language supports offered in secondary schools.
9. Authors (Clanfield et al., 2014; Parekh, Killoran, and Crawford, 2011) also argue that the notions of disability and exceptionality have expanded to include a much larger segment of the student population over the last five or six decades, and that poor and minority students are overrepresented in these groups, leading to placement in programs and streams that offer fewer academic opportunities.
10. Although they are frequently described as "stay-in-school" programs, high school apprenticeship programs in Alberta primarily attract students who are average in terms of academic performance and have very clear career goals. High academic achievers seldom apply and lower achieving students do not meet the entrance criteria related to attainment (being on track to graduate) and attendance.
11. This does not include students who do not self-report Aboriginal identity and students who left high school in Grades 10 or 11.
12. My co-investigator on the "Tracking High School Apprentices" study was Dr. Wolfgang Lehmann. Dr. Milosh Raykov analyzed the survey data and Zane Hamm

was involved as a research assistant. Our data included an online survey completed by 173 participants and 111 in-depth interviews (56 from Alberta and 55 from Ontario) conducted between 2009 and 2011.

13. Harris and Simons (2005) present these factors in discussing apprenticeship retention in Australia.

14. The top six RAP trades, in terms of student registrations, were welder, heavy equipment technician, automotive service technician, electrician, carpenter, and hairstylist (Alberta Apprenticeship and Industry Training Board, 2010). In Ontario, the top six trades, in terms of student enrolments, were auto service technician, cook, electrician, carpenter, machinist, and hairstylist (Personal communication, Ministry of Training, Colleges and Universities 2007).

15. All interview participant names are pseudonyms.

References

Aboriginal Learning Knowledge Centre. (2009). *Synthesis report of the Aboriginal Learning Knowledge Centre's literature reviews: Responsive educational systems*. Retrieved from http://www.ccl-cca.ca/aboriginallearning

Akkerman, S., & Bakker, A. (2011). Boundary crossing and boundary objects. *Journal of Educational Research, 81*(2), 132–69.

Alberta Apprenticeship and Industry Training Board. (2010). *Annual report 2009–2010*. Retrieved from http://tradesecrets.alberta.ca/sources/pdfs/board_publications/annual _reports/BOARD_ANN_REP09-10.PDF

Alberta Education. (1984). *Review of secondary programs*. Edmonton, CA.

Alberta Education. (1991). *Vision for the Nineties: A plan of action*. Edmonton, CA.

Alberta Education. (1994). *Meeting the challenge: Three-year business plan for education*. Edmonton, CA.

Alberta Education. (1996). *Framework for enhancing business involvement in education*. Edmonton, CA.

Alberta Education. (1998). *Career and technology studies: Manual for administrators, counselors and teachers*. Edmonton: CA.

Alberta Education. (2010). *Inspiring education*. Edmonton, CA.

Alberta Learning. (2001). *Removing barriers to high school completion*. Retrieved from http://ideas.education.alberta.ca/media/4327/barrierreport.pdf

Andersen, E. (2012, May 5). Can Canada's schools pass the next great intelligence test? *The Globe and Mail*. Retrieved from http://www.theglobeandmail.com/news/ national/time-to-lead/can-canadas-schools-pass-the-next-great-intelligence-test/ article4591606/

Anderson, B. (2010). Migration, immigration controls and the fashioning of precarious workers. *Work, Employment and Society, 24*(2), 300–17.

Anft, M. (2013, November 11). The STEM crisis: Reality or myth? *Chronicle of Higher Education*. Retrieved from http://chronicle.com/article/The-STEM-Crisis -Reality-or/142879/

Arendt, H. (1958). *The human condition*. Chicago: University of Chicago Press.

Association of Universities and Colleges of Canada. (2011). *Trends in higher education. Volume 1 – enrolment*. Retrieved from http://www.aucc.ca/wp-content/uploads/2011/ 05/trends-2011-vol1-enrolment-e.pdf

Avis, J. (2004). Work-based learning and social justice: "Learning to labour" and the new vocationalism in England. *Journal of Education and Work, 17*(2), 197–217.

Ball, S. (2003). *Class strategies and the education market: The middle classes and social advantage*. London, UK: Routledge Falmer.

Barman, J. (2012). Schooled for inequality: The education of BC Aboriginal children. In S. Burke and P. Milewski (Eds), *Schooling in transition* (pp. 255–76). Toronto, ON: University of Toronto Press.

Bartlett, C. (2012a, November 8). Starting trades training in grade 10 means no student debt for this teen. *Edmonton Journal*. Retrieved from http://www.edmonton journal.com/business/tradesalberta/Starting+trades+training+Grade+means+ student/7520552/story.html

Bartlett, C. (2012b, November 8). Hesitant parents warm up to idea of their children going into trades. *Edmonton Journal*. Retrieved from http://www.edmontonjournal.

com/business/tradesalberta/Hesitant+parents+warm+idea+their+children+going/7520578/story.html

Bascaramurty, D. (2011, July 19). Unpaid interns: Working for free. *The Globe and Mail.* Retrieved from http://www.theglobeandmail.com/globe-investor/personal-finance/unpaid-interns-working-for-free/article590498/

Bauder, H. (2003). "Brain abuse" or the devaluation of immigrant labour in Canada. *Antipode, 35*(4), 699–717.

BC Ministry of Education. (2011). *BC's education plan.* Victoria, BC.

BC Ministry of Education. (2015). *BC's education plan: Focus on learning, January 2015 update.* Victoria, BC.

Beach, K. (1999). Beyond transitions: A sociocultural expedition beyond transfer in education. *Review of Research in Education, 24*(1), 101–39.

Beck, U. (1992) *Risk society: Towards a new modernity.* London, UK: Sage.

Becker, G. (1964). *Human capital.* Chicago: University of Chicago Press.

Beckstead, D., & Vinodrai, T. (2003). *Dimensions of occupational changes in Canada's knowledge economy, 1971–1996.* Retrieved from http://www.publications.gc.ca/site/archivee-archived.html?url=http://www.publications.gc.ca/Collection/Statcan/11-622-M/11-622-MIE2003004.pdf

Bell, D. (2004). Canada passes the Technical and Vocational Training Assistance Act, 1960. In D. Schugurensky (Ed.), *History of education: Selected moments of the 20th century.* Unpublished manuscript, Department of Adult Education and Counselling Psychology, The Ontario Institute for Studies in Education of the University of Toronto (OISE/UT). Retrieved from http://schugurensky.faculty.asu.edu/moments/1960TVTAA.html

Bell, D., & Benes, K. (2012). *Transitioning graduates to work: Improving the labour-market success of poorly integrated new entrants (PINES) in Canada.* Ottawa, ON: Canadian Career Development Foundation.

Bell, D., & Bezanson, L. (2006). *Career development services for Canadian youth: Access, adequacy and accountability.* Pathways to the Labour Market Series – No. 1. Ottawa, ON: Canadian Policy Research Networks and the Canadian Career Development Foundation.

Benson, C. (1997). New vocationalism in the United States: Potential problems and outlook. *Economics of Education Review, 16*(3), 201–12.

Berrett, B., & Hoover, E. (2015, February 5). College freshmen seek financial security amid emotional insecurity. *The Chronicle of Higher Education.* Retrieved from http://chronicle.com/article/College-Freshmen-Seek/151645/

Betcherman, G., McMullen, K., & Davidman, K. (1998). *Training for the New Economy.* Canadian Policy Research Networks. Retrieved from http://www.cprn.org/doc.cfm?l=en&doc=453

Billett, S. (2014). The standing of vocational education: Sources of its societal esteem and implications for its enactment. *Journal of Vocational Education and Training, 66*(1), 1–21.

Bills, D. (2009). Vocationalism. In A. Furlong (Ed.), *Handbook of youth and young adulthood: New perspectives and agendas* (pp. 127–34). Abingdon, UK: Routledge.

Boothby, D., & Drewes, T. (2006). Postsecondary education in Canada: Returns to university, college and trades education. *Canadian Public Policy, 32*(1), 1–21.

Bourdieu, P. (1989). Social space and symbolic power. *Sociological Theory, 7*(1), 14–25.

Bowlby, J., & McMullen, K. (2002). *At a crossroads: First results of the 18 to 20-year-old cohort of the Youth in Transition survey.* Statistics Canada. Retrieved from http://publications.gc.ca/Collection/Statcan/81-591-X/81-591-XIE2000001.pdf

Brant Castellano, M. (2008). Reflections on identity and empowerment: Recurring themes in the discourse on and with Aboriginal youth. *Horizons, 10*(1), 7–12.

Brisbois, R. (2003). *How Canada stacks up: The quality of work—an international perspective*. Canadian Policy Research Networks. Retrieved from http://www.cprn.org/documents/25597_en.pdf

Brisbois, R., Orton, L., & Saunders, R. (2008). *Connecting supply and demand in Canada's youth labour market*. Pathways to the Labour Market Series – No. 8. Canadian Policy Research Networks. Retrieved from http://www.cprn.org/documents/49679_EN.pdf

Broadbent Institute. (2014). *Time for a new deal for young people*. Ottawa, ON.

Brown, P. (1987). *Schooling ordinary kids: Inequality, unemployment and the new vocationalism*. London, UK: Routledge.

Brown, P. (2000). The globalisation of positional competition. *Sociology, 34*(4), 633–53.

Brown, P. (2006). The opportunity trap. In H. Lauder, P. Brown, J. Dillabough, & R. Halsey (Eds), *Education, globalization and social change* (pp. 381–97). Oxford, UK: Oxford University Press.

Brown, P., & Lauder, H. (2006). Globalization, knowledge and the myth of the magnet economy. *Globalisation, Societies and Education, 4*(1), 25–57.

Brown, P., Lauder, H., & Ashton, D. (2011). *The global auction: The broken promises of education, jobs and incomes*. Oxford, UK: Oxford University Press.

Bryce, R. (1970). The Technical and Vocational Training Assistance Act of 1916–17: An historical survey and documentary analysis. (Unpublished doctoral dissertation). University of Alberta, Edmonton, AB.

Bullen, J. (1989). Children of the industrial age: Children, work and welfare in late nineteenth-century Ontario. (Unpublished doctoral dissertation). University of Ottawa, Ottawa, ON.

Canadian Apprenticeship Forum. (2013, Oct 10). *Apprenticeship analysis: Youth perceptions of careers in the skilled trades*. Retrieved from http://caf-fca.org/

Canadian Chamber of Commerce. (2014, October 14). *A battle we can't afford to lose: Getting young Canadians from education to employment*. Retrieved from http://www.chamber.ca/media/blog/141014-a-battle-we-cant-afford-to-lose-getting-young-canadians-from-education-to-employment/

Canadian Education Statistics Council. (2014). *Education indicators in Canada: An international perspective 2014*. Statistics Canada. Retrieved from http://www.statcan.gc.ca/pub/81-604-x/2014001/hl-fs-eng.htm

Canadian Labour Congress. (2012, February 14). Submission by the Canadian Labour Congress to the Department of Foreign Affairs and International Trade regarding consultations on potential free trade agreement negotiations with trans-Pacific partnership members. Retrieved from http://www.progressive-economics.ca/wp-content/uploads/2012/02/CLC-TPP.pdf

Canadian Press. (2012, September 2). *Unions on decline in private sector: Unionized workers' salaries lagging behind non-unionized workers, Conference Board says*. CBC News. Retrieved from http://www.cbc.ca/news/canada/story/2012/09/02/unions-labour-canada-decline.html

Canadian Services Coalition & Canadian Chamber of Commerce. (2006). *Canadian services sector: A new success story*. Ottawa, ON.

Centre for Contemporary Cultural Studies. (1981). *Unpopular education: Schooling and social democracy in Britain since 1944*. London, UK: Hutchinson.

Clanfield, D., Curtis, B., Galabuzi, G., San Vicente, A., Livingstone, D.W., & Smaller, H. (2014). *Restacking the deck: Streaming by class, race and gender in Ontario schools*. Ottawa, ON: Canadian Centre for Policy Alternatives.

Clarke, L., & Winch, C. (2004). Apprenticeship and applied theoretical knowledge. *Educational Philosophy and Theory, 36*(5), 509–22.

Collins, R. (1979). *The credential society.* New York, NY: Academic Press.

Commission on Educational Planning. (1972). *The Worth Report: A choice of futures.* Edmonton, AB: Queen's Printer for the Province of Alberta.

Conference Board of Canada. (2005, December). *Changing employers' behavior about training.* Issue statement. Ottawa.

Conference Board of Canada. (2013). *The need to make skills work: The cost of Ontario's skills gap.* Ottawa: Conference Board. Retrieved from http://www.conferenceboard.ca/e-library/abstract.aspx?did=5563

Council of Ontario Universities. (2014). *Experiential learning report: Bringing life to learning at Ontario universities.* Retrieved from http://cou.on.ca/publications/reports/pdfs/march262014---experiential-learning-report

Coupland, D. (1991). *Generation X: Tales for an accelerated culture.* New York, NY: St Martin's Press.

Crouch, C., & Streeck, W. (2006). *The diversity of democracy: Corporatism, social order and political conflict.* Cheltenham, UK: Edward Elgar.

Curriculum Development Branch, Alberta Education. (1989, June). *Proposed directions for change: A vision for practical arts programs in secondary schools in Alberta.* Edmonton, AB: Alberta Education.

Curriculum Policies Board, Alberta Education. (1977). *Alberta education and diploma requirements.* Edmonton, AB: Alberta Education.

Curtis, B., Livingstone, D.W., & Smaller, H. (1992). *Stacking the deck: The streaming of working-class kids in Ontario schools.* Toronto, ON: Our Schools/Our Selves.

Dauvergne, C., & Marsden, S. (2014). The ideology of temporary labour migration in the post-global era. *Citizenship Studies, 18*(2), 224–42.

Davies, S., & Guppy, N. (2014). *The schooled society: An introduction to the sociology of education* (3rd ed.). Don Mills, ON: Oxford University Press.

de Broucker, P. (2005). *Without a paddle: What to do about Canada's young drop-outs.* Ottawa, ON: Canadian Policy Research Networks.

Dei, G., Mazucca, J., McIsaac, E., & Zine, J. (1997). *Reconstructing 'drop-out': A critical ethnography of the dynamics of black students' disengagement from school.* Toronto, ON: University of Toronto Press.

Deissinger, T., Aff, J., Fuller, A., & Jorgensen, C. (Eds). (2013). *Hybrid qualifications: Structures and problems in the context of European VET policy.* Bern, Switzerland: Peter Lang.

Dennison, J.D., & Gallagher, P. (1986). *Canada's community colleges: A critical analysis.* Vancouver: University of British Columbia Press.

Doray, P., Ménard, L., & Adouane, A. (2008). *Implementing the school-to-work transition in Québec.* Canadian Policy Research Networks. Retrieved from http://www.cprn.org/documents/49520_EN.pdf

Drost, W. (1977). Social efficiency reexamined: The Dewey-Snedden controversy. *Curriculum Inquiry, 7*(1), 19–32.

Dwyer, P., & Wyn, J. (2001). *Youth, education and risk.* London, UK: Routledge/Falmer.

Economic Council of Canada. (1992). *A Lot to Learn: Education and Training in Canada: A statement.* Ottawa, ON: Economic Council of Canada.

Ellis, J., & Axelrod, P. (Forthcoming, 2016). Continuity and change in special education policy development in Toronto public schools, 1945 to the present. *Teachers College Record.*

Finnie, R., Childs, S., Pavlic, D., & Jevtovic, N. (2014, November 21). How much do university graduates earn? Education Policy Research Initiative, Research Brief 3, University of Ottawa. Retrieved from http://socialsciences.uottawa.ca/irpe-epri/eng/documents/EPRIBRIEF3OverallGradEarnings.pdf

Fisher, D., Rubenson, K., Bernatchez, J., Clift, R., Jones, G., Lee, J., MacIvor, M., Meredith, J., Shanahan, T., & Trottier, C. (2006). *Canadian federal policy and postsecondary education.* (Report). Vancouver, BC: Centre for Policy Studies in Higher Education and Training and Alliance for International Higher Education Policy Studies. Retrieved from http://www.forschungsnetzwerk.at/downloadpub/chet2452487040.pdf

Fortin, N., & Parent, D. (2008). *Employee training in Canada.* Canadian Labour Market and Skills Researcher Network (Working paper No. 3). Retrieved from http://www.clsrn.econ.ubc.ca/workingpapers/ES%20-%20CLSRN%20Working%20Paper%20no.%203%20-%20Fortin%20&%20Parent%20-%20Final.pdf

Foster, J. (2012). Making temporary permanent: the silent transformation of the Temporary Foreign Workers Program. *Just Labour, 19,* 22–46.

Freeman, S. (2007). *The intersection of policy and practice in one stand-alone vocational school: The ABC story.* (Unpublished doctoral dissertation). Ontario Institute for Studies in Education, Toronto, ON.

Friese, L. (2012, August 29). Why are we training our arts grads to be baristas? *The Globe and Mail.* Retrieved from http://www.theglobeandmail.com/report-on-business/economy/canada-competes/why-are-we-training-our-arts-grads-to-be-baristas/article4507579/

Fuller, A., & Unwin, L. (2006). Expansive and restrictive learning environments. In K. Evans, P. Hodkinson, H. Rainbird, and L. Unwin (Eds), *Improving workplace learning* (pp. 27–48). London, UK: Routledge.

Fuller, S., & Vosko, L. (2008). Temporary employment and social inequality in Canada. *Social Indicators Research, 88,* 31–50.

Galarneau, D., Morisette, R., & Usalcas, J. (2013). *What has changed for young people in Canada?* Statistics Canada Catalogue no. 75-006-X. Ottawa, ON: Minister of Industry.

Gaskell, J. (1992). *Gender matters from school to work.* Toronto, ON: OISE Press.

Gaskell, J., Nicol, C., & Tsai, L. (2004). Working outcomes in the classroom: A case study of applied academics in British Columbia. In J. Gaskell and K. Rubenson (Eds), *Educational outcomes for the Canadian workplace: New frameworks for policy and research* (pp. 186–203). Toronto, ON: University of Toronto Press.

Gaskell, J., & Rubenson, K. (2004). Introduction. In J. Gaskell and K. Rubenson (Eds), *Educational outcomes for the Canadian workplace* (pp. 3-17). Toronto, ON: University of Toronto Press.

Gidney, R. (1999). *From hope to Harris: The reshaping of Ontario's schools.* Toronto, ON: University of Toronto Press.

Gleeson, D., and Keep, E. (2004). Voice without accountability: The changing relationship between employers, the state, and education in England. *Oxford Review of Education, 30*(1), 37–63.

Godsey, M. (2015, February 17). School is about more than training kids to be adults: What teachers risk when they focus only on ensuring kids are ready for college and their careers. *The Atlantic.* Retrieved from http://www.theatlantic.com/education/archive/2015/02/school-is-about-more-than-training-kids-to-be-adults/385475/

Goldenberg, M. (2006). *Employer investment in workplace learning in Canada.* Discussion paper prepared by Canadian Policy Research Networks. Retrieved from http://

www.ccl-cca.ca/NR/rdonlyres/4F86830F-D201-4CAF-BA12-333B51CEB988/0/
EmployerInvestmentWorkplaceLearningCCLCPRN.pdf

Government of Alberta. (2010). *Inspiring education: A dialogue with Albertans.* (Steering Committee Report). Retrieved from https://ideas.education.alberta.ca/media/14847/inspiring%20education%20steering%20committee%20report.pdf

Government of Canada. (2002). *Knowledge matters: Skills and learning for Canadians.* Retrieved from http://publications.gc.ca/site/eng/108190/publication.html

Government of Canada. (2014, October 4). "Harper government celebrates most successful month for trade and investment in Canadian history." Retrieved from http://www.international.gc.ca/media/comm/news-communiques/2014/10/01a.aspx?lang=eng

Government of Ontario Program Pathways for Students at Risk Work Group. (2003). *Building pathways to success. Grades 7 to 12.* (Final report). Retrieved from http://publications.gc.ca/site/eng/108190/publication.html

Gradwell, J. (1999). A Canadian perspective on vocational education and training. In A. Pautler (Ed.), *Workforce education: Issues for the new century* (pp. 241–52). Ann Arbor, MI: Prakken Publications.

Green, A., & Janmaat, J. (2011). *Regimes of social cohesion.* Basingstoke, UK: Palgrave Macmillan.

Grubb, W.N. (1996). The new vocationalism: What it is, what it could be. *Phi Delta Kappan, 77*(8), 535–66.

Grubb, W.N. (2006). *Vocational education and training: Issues for a thematic review.* Paris, France: OECD.

Guile, D. (2010). *The learning challenge of the knowledge economy.* Rotterdam, Netherlands: Sense Publishers.

Guile, D., & Griffiths, T. (2001). Learning through work experience. *Journal of Education and Work, 14*(1), 113–31.

Guile, D., & Young, M. (2003). Transfer and transition in vocational education: Some theoretical considerations. In T. Tuomi-Grohn and Y. Engestrom (Eds), *Between school and work: New perspectives on transfer and boundary-crossing* (pp. 63–81). Amsterdam, Netherlands: Pergamon.

Gunderson, M. (1989). Harmonization of labour policies under trade liberalization. *Industrial Relations, 53*(1), 24–54.

Haasler, S., and Gottschall, G. (2015). Still a perfect model? The gender impact of vocational training in Germany. *Journal of Vocational Education & Training, 67*(1): 78–92.

Hager, P., & Hyland, T. (2003). Vocational education and training. *Education: Book Chapters* (Paper 5). Open access provided by University of Bolton Institutional Repository. Retrieved from http://digitalcommons.bolton.ac.uk/ed_chapters/5

Hall, P., & Soskice, D. (2001). *Varieties of capitalism: The institutional foundations of comparative advantage.* Oxford, UK: Oxford University Press.

Hallam, S., & Ireson, J. (2007). Secondary school pupils' satisfaction with their ability grouping placements. *British Educational Research Journal, 33*(1), 27–45.

Halliday, D. (2012, November 8). Careers: The Next Generation promotes trades careers to youth in Alberta: Non-profit organization tackles skilled labour shortage. *Edmonton Journal.* Retrieved from http://www.edmontonjournal.com/business/trades-alberta/Careers+Next+Generation+promotes+trades+careers/7519324/story.html

Hango, D., & de Broucker, P. (2007). *Education to labour market pathways of Canadian youth: Findings from the Youth in Transition Survey.* (Report prepared for Canadian Policy Research Networks). Statistics Canada. Retrieved from http://www.statcan.gc.ca/pub/81-595-m/81-595-m2007054-eng.htm

Harris, R., & M. Simons. (2005.) Exploring the notion of retention in apprenticeship. *Education and Training, 47*(4/5), 350–65.

Harvey, D. (2005). *A brief history of neoliberalism.* Oxford, UK: Oxford University Press.

Hayward, G. (2004). A century of vocationalism. *Oxford Review of Education, 30*(1), 3–12.

Heinz, W. (2000). Youth transitions and employment in Germany. *International Social Science Journal, 164,* 161–70.

Heinz, W. (2003). The restructuring of work and the modernization of vocational training in Germany. In H. Schuetze and R. Sweet (Eds), *Integrating school and workplace learning in Canada* (pp. 25–43). Montreal, QC: McGill-Queen's University Press.

Heinz, W., & Taylor, A. (2005). Learning and work transition policies in comparative perspective: Canada and Germany. In K. Leithwood, D. Livingstone, A. Cumming, N. Bascia, & A. Datnow (Eds), *International handbook of educational policy, Volume 2* (pp. 847–64). New York, NY: Kluwer.

Helms Jorgensen, C. (2010, September). Hybrid qualifications: Country report Denmark. Leonardo Project. Retrieved from http://hq-lll.eu/presentations/reports2010/Country%20Report%20Denmark%20September%202010.pdf

Heron, C. (1986). Hamilton steelworkers and the rise of mass production. In B. Palmer (Ed.), *The character of class struggle* (pp. 68–89). Toronto, ON: McClelland & Stewart.

Hickox, M. (1995). Situating vocationalism. *British Journal of Sociology of Education, 16*(2), 153– 163.

Hodgson, A., & Spours, K. (Eds). (1997). *Dearing and beyond: 14–19 qualifications, frameworks and systems.* London, UK: Kogan Page.

Hoffman, N., Vargas, J., Venezia, A., and Miller, M. (Eds). (2007). *Minding the gap: Why integrating high school with college makes sense and how to do it.* Cambridge, MA: Harvard University Press.

Hudson, J., & Taylor, A. (2011). Career pathways in health services: Report of 2010 survey data for student interns. (Report prepared for CAREERS the Next Generation). Edmonton, AB.

Huffbauer, G., & Schott, J. (2005). *NAFTA revisited: Achievements and challenges.* Washington, DC: Institute for International Economics.

Hunter, J. (2013, October 27). B.C. eyes boosting trades in curriculum overhaul. *The Globe and Mail.* Retrieved from http://www.theglobeandmail.com/news/british-columbia/bc-eyes-boosting-trades-in-curriculum-overhaul/article15108656/#dashboard/follows/

Hyslop-Margison, E. (2001). An assessment of the historical arguments in vocational education reform. *Journal of Career and Technical Education, 17*(1). Retrieved from http://scholar.lib.vt.edu/ejournals/JCTE/v17n1/hyslop.html

Katherine. (2013, September 18). I'm a millennial. Please stop being a douche to me [Weblog post]. Retrieved from http://iambeggingmymothernottoreadthisblog.com/2013/09/18/im-a-millenial-please-stop-being-a-douche-to-me/

International Labor Organization. (2013). *Global employment trends for youth 2013: A generation at risk.* Geneva, Switzerland: International Labour Office. Retrieved from http://www.ilo.org/global/research/global-reports/global-employment-trends/youth/2013/lang--en/index.htm

Jackson, N. (1993). Rethinking vocational learning. In R. Coulter and I. Goodson (Eds), *Rethinking vocationalism* (pp. 166–80). Toronto, ON: Our Schools/Our Selves.

Jackson, N., & Gaskell, J. (1987). White collar vocationalism: The rise of commercial education in Ontario and British Columbia, 1870–1920. *Curriculum Inquiry, 17*(2), 177–201.

Karp, E. (1988). *The drop-out phenomenon in Ontario secondary schools: A report to the Ontario study of the relevance of education and the issue of dropouts.* Toronto, ON: Ministry of Education.

Keep, E., & Payne, J. (2002) Policy interventions for a vibrant work-based route—or when policy hits reality's fan (again). In K. Evans, P. Hodkinson, & L. Unwin (Eds), *Working to learn: Transforming learning in the workplace* (pp. 187– 211). London, UK: Kogan Page.

Kenway, J., & Bullen, E. (2001). *Consuming children.* Buckingham, UK: Open University Press.

Kim, K. (2010). *NAFTA is a good deal for workers in North America: Theories and evidence.* Proceedings of the Northeast Business and Economics Association (pp. 517–22). Morristown, NJ: Northeast Business and Economics Association.

Kincheloe, J. (1999). *How do we tell the workers?: The socioeconomic foundations of work and vocational education.* Boulder, CO: Westview.

King, A. (2004). *Double cohort study: phase 3.* (Report prepared for the Ontario Ministry of Education). Kingston, ON: Queen's University.

King, A., Warren, W., Boyer, J., & Chin, P. (2005). *Double cohort study: Phase 4.* (Report prepared for the Ontario Ministry of Education by Social Program Evaluation Group). Kingston, ON: Queen's University.

King, A., Warren, W., King, M., Brook, J., & Kocher, P. (2009). *Who doesn't go to post-secondary education?* (Final report of findings for Colleges Ontario, Collaborative Research Project). Kingston, ON.

Kitigawa, K. (1998). *Ontario's secondary school and apprenticeship reforms.* Ottawa, ON: Conference Board of Canada.

Knight, C. (2012). Black parents speak: Education in mid-nineteenth-century Canada West. In S. Burke & P. Milewski (Eds), *Schooling in transition* (pp. 225–36). Toronto, ON: University of Toronto Press.

Krahn, H. (1991). The changing Canadian labour market. In D. Ashton & G. Lowe (Eds), *Making their way: Education, training and the labour market in Canada and Britain* (pp. 15–37). Buckingham, UK: Open University Press.

Krahn, H., & Hudson, J. (2006). *Pathways of Alberta youth through the post-secondary system into the labour market, 1996–2003.* Report prepared for Canadian Policy Research Networks. Ottawa, ON.

Krahn, H., Lowe, G., & Hughes, K. (2011). *Work, industry, and Canadian society* (6th ed.). Toronto, ON: Nelson.

Krahn, H., & Taylor, A. (2005). Resilient teenagers: Explaining the high educational aspirations of visible minority immigrant youth in Canada. *Journal of International Migration and Integration, 6*(3/4), 405–34.

Lackey, L. (2004). Policy, rhetoric, and educational outcomes: Interpreting skills now! In J. Gaskell and K. Rubenson (Eds), *Educational outcomes for the Canadian workplace* (pp. 159–85). Toronto, ON: University of Toronto Press.

Lam, E. (2010, Nov 26). Contract work on rise in Canada. *Postmedia News.* Retrieved from http://login.ezproxy.library.ualberta.ca/login?url=http://search.proquest.com/docview/849243757?accountid=14474

Larner, W. (2000). Neoliberalism: Policy, ideology, governmentality. *Studies in Political Economy, 63,* 5–25.

Law Commission of Ontario (2012). *Vulnerable workers and precarious work.* (Interim report). Retrieved from http://www.lco-cdo.org/en/vulnerable-workers-interim-report

Lazerson, M., & Dunn, T. (1977). Schools and the work crisis: Vocationalism in Canadian education. In H. Stevenson and D. Wilson (Eds), *Precepts, policy and process: Perspectives on contemporary Canadian education* (pp. 285–303). London, UK: Alexander Blake Associates.

Lehmann, W. (2000). Is Germany's dual system still a model for Canadian youth apprenticeship initiatives? *Canadian Public Policy, 26*(2), 225– 240.

Lehmann, W. (2007). *Choosing to labour? School–work transitions and social class*. Montreal, QC: McGill-Queen's University Press.

Lehmann, W. (2012). Working-class students, habitus, and the development of student roles: A Canadian case study. *British Journal of Sociology of Education, 33*(4), 527–46.

Lehmann, W., & Taylor, A. (2003). Giving employers what they want? New vocationalism in Alberta. *Journal of Education and Work, 16*(1), 45–67.

Lehmann, W., Taylor, A., & Hamm, Z. (2013). "Go west young man!" Youth apprenticeship and opportunity structures in two Canadian provinces. *Journal of Education and Work, 28*(1), 44–65.

Lehmann, W., Taylor, A., & Wright, L. (2014 online). Youth Apprenticeships in Canada: On their inferior status despite skilled labour shortages. *Journal of Vocational Education and Training, 66*(4), 572–89. doi:10.1080/13636820.2014.958868

Lewchuk, W., de Wolff, A., & King, A. (2007). Employment strain, precarious employment, and temporary employment agencies. In V. Shalla and W. Clement (Eds), *Work in Tumultuous Times* (pp. 98–130). Montreal, QC: McGill-Queen's University Press.

Livingstone, D.W. (1994). Searching for missing links: neo-Marxist theories of education, in L. Erwin and D. MacLennan (Eds), *Sociology of Education in Canada* (pp. 55–82). Toronto, ON: Copp Clark Longman.

Livingstone, D.W. (1999). *The education–jobs gap: Underemployment or economic democracy*. Toronto, ON: Garamond.

Livingstone, D.W. (Ed.). (2009). *Education and jobs: Exploring the gaps*. Toronto, ON: University of Toronto Press.

Livingstone, D.W. (2010). Job requirements and workers' learning: Formal gaps, informal closure, systemic limits. *Journal of Education and Work, 23*(3): 207–31.

Livingstone, D., and Scholtz, A. (2007). Contradictions of labour processes and workers' use of skills in advanced capitalist economies. In V. Shalla and W. Clement (Eds), *Work in tumultuous times* (pp. 131–62). Montreal, QC: McGill-Queen's University Press.

Lloyd, C. (1985). John Seath and the development of vocational education in Ontario, 1890–1920. (Unpublished doctoral dissertation). Toronto, ON: University of Toronto.

Looker, D., & Dwyer, P. (1998). Education and negotiated reality: Complexities facing rural youth in the 1990s. *Journal of Youth Studies, 1*(1): 5–22.

Lyons, J., Randhawa, B., & Paulson, N. (1991). The development of vocational education in Canada. *Canadian Journal of Education, 16*(2), 137–50.

McCrea Silva, M., & Phillips, S. M. (2007). *Trading up—High school and beyond: Five illustrative Canadian case studies*. (Pathways to the Labour Market Series No. 4). Ottawa, ON: Canadian Policy Research Networks.

Macdonald, D., & Shaker, E. (2012). *Eduflation and the high cost of learning*. Canadian Centre for Policy Alternatives. Retrieved from http://www.policyalternatives.ca/sites/default/files/uploads/publications/National%20Office/2012/09/Eduflation%20and%20High%20Cost%20Learning.pdf

McFarland, J. (2012, Sep 25). Same job, less pay: The return of two-tier wage scales. *The Globe and Mail*. Retrieved from http://login.ezproxy.library.ualberta.ca/login?url=http://search.proquest.com/docview/1069320772?accountid=14474

McInturff, K. (2013, April). Behind the numbers: Closing Canada's gender gap. Ottawa, ON: Canadian Centre for Policy Alternatives. Retrieved from http://

www.policyalternatives.ca/sites/default/files/uploads/publications/National%20 Office/2013/04/Closing_Canadas_Gender_Gap_0.pdf

Manzer, R. (1994). *Public schools and political ideas: Canadian educational policy in histori-cal perspective.* Toronto, ON: University of Toronto Press.

Marginson, S. (1997). *Markets in education.* St. Leonards, Australia: Allen and Unwin.

Marks, L. (1986). *Kale meydelach* or *shulamith* girls: Cultural change and continuity among Jewish parents and daughters—A case study of Toronto's Harbord Collegiate Institute in the 1920s. *Canadian Woman Studies, 7*(3), 85–89.

Marquardt, R. (1998). *Enter at your own risk: Canadian youth and the labour market.* Toronto, ON: Between the Lines.

Martell, G. (2009, February). It's the bottom streaming that matters most [web log post]. Retrieved from http://educationactiontoronto.com/archive/it-s-the-bottom -streaming-that-matters-most

Mazurek, K. (1999). Passing fancies: Educational changes in Alberta. In T. Harrison & J. Kachur (Eds), *Contested classrooms* (pp. 3–20). Edmonton, AB: University of Alberta Press and Parkland Institute.

Méhaut, P. (2012). Three challenges for the VET system: The end or rebirth of vocational education. In S. Stolz & P. Gonon (Eds), *Challenges and reforms in vocational educa-tion: Aspects of inclusion and exclusion* (pp. 73–93). Bern, Switzerland: Peter Lang.

Milan, A., & Tran, K. (2004). Blacks in Canada: A long history. *Canadian Social Trends* (Statistics Canada Catalogue No. 11-008).

Miner, R. (2010). *People without jobs, jobs without people: Ontario's labour market future.* Toronto, ON: Miner Management Consultants.

Ministry of Education. (2005). *The Ontario curriculum, grades 9 and 10: Mathematics.* Retrieved from http://www.edu.gov.on.ca/eng/curriculum/secondary/math910curr.pdf

Ministry of Education. (2007). *The Ontario curriculum, grades 11 and 12: Mathematics.* Retrieved from https://www.edu.gov.on.ca/eng/curriculum/secondary/math1112 currb.pdf

Ministry of Education, Program Pathways for Students at Risk Work Group. (2003). *Building pathways to success, Grades 7–12.* (Report). Retrieved from http://www.edu. gov.on.ca/eng/document/reports/pathways.html

Mjelde, L. (1987). From hand to mind. In D. Livingstone (Ed), *Critical pedagogy and cultural power* (pp. 205–21). Toronto, ON: Garamond.

Molgat, M., Deschenaux, F., & LeBlanc, P. (2011). Vocational education in Canada: Do policy directions and youth trajectories always meet? *Journal of Vocational Education and Training, 63*(4), 505–24.

Moore, R. (2009). *Towards the sociology of truth.* London, UK: Continuum.

Moore, R., & Young, M. (2001). Knowledge and the curriculum in the sociology of education: Towards a re-conceptualisation. *British Journal of Sociology of Education, 22*(4), 445–61.

Morrison, T. (1974). Reform as social tracking: The case of industrial education in Ontario 1870–1900. *Journal of Educational Thought, 8,* 87–110.

Oakes, J., & Lipton, M. (2007). *Teaching to change the world* (2nd edn). Boston, MA: McGraw-Hill.

O'Donnell, S. (2013, May 6). Province plans more dual-credit courses for high school students. *Edmonton Journal.* Retrieved from http://www.edmontonjournal.com/news/ Province+plans+more+dual+credit+courses+high+school+students/8344027/story. html

OECD. (2000a). *The service economy.* (Business and industry policy forum series). Paris, France: OECD.

OECD. (2000b). *From initial education to working life: Making transitions work.* Paris, France: OECD.

OECD. (2008). *Jobs for youth: Canada.* Retrieved from http://www.oecd.org/els/40808376.pdf

OECD. (2009). *Tackling the job crisis: The labour market and social policy response. Helping youth to get a firm foothold in the labour market.* (OECD Labour and Employment Ministerial meeting). Paris, France. Retrieved from http://www.oecd.org/employment/ministerial/43766254.pdf

OECD & International Labour Organization (ILO). (2011). *Giving youth a better start.* (Policy note for the G20 Meeting of Labour and Employment Ministers). Paris, France.

Ontario Department of Education (1968). Living and Learning: The Report of the Provincial Committee on Aims and Objectives of Education in the Schools of Ontario. Toronto: Ontario.

Ontario. (1995). Royal Commission on Learning. For the Love of Learning: Report of the Royal Commission on Learning. 4 vols. Toronto: Queen's Printer for Ontario.

Ontario Premier's Council. (1990). *People and skills in the new economy.* Toronto, Ontario.

Ore, J. (2012, September 2). What does Labour Day mean to you? [web log]. *CBC News,* community blog. Retrieved from http://www.cbc.ca/news/yourcommunity/2012/09/what-does-labour-day-mean-to-you.html

Osborne, D., & Gaebler, T. (1993). *Reinventing government.* New York, NY: Plume.

Ovsey, D. (2013, June 6). Should Canada have a national education and training strategy? *Financial Post.* Retrieved from http://business.financialpost.com/executive/should-canada-have-a-national-education-and-training-strategy

Palmer, B. (1983). *Working-class experience: The rise and reconstitution of Canadian labour, 1800–1980.* Toronto, ON: Butterworth.

Parekh, G., Killoran, I., & Crawford, C. (2011). The Toronto connection: Poverty, perceived ability, and access to education equity. *Canadian Journal of Education, 34*(3), 249–79.

Perlin, R. (2012). *Intern nation: How to earn nothing and learn little in the brave new economy.* London, UK: Verso.

Phythian, K., Walters, D., & Anisef, P. (2009). Entry class and the early employment experience of immigrants in Canada. *Canadian Studies in Population, 36*(3–4), 363–82.

Polanyi, M. (1966). *Tacit knowledge.* New York, NY: Doubleday.

Pring, R. (2004). The skills revolution. *Oxford Review of Education, 30*(1): 105–16.

Radwanski, G. (1987). *Ontario study of the relevance of education, and the issue of dropouts.* Toronto, ON: Ministry of Education.

Raffe, D., Howieson, C., Spours, K., & Young, M. (1998). The unification of post-compulsory education: Towards a conceptual framework. *British Journal of Educational Studies, 46*(2), 169–87.

Raja, M., Beaujot, R., & Woldemicael, G. (2012). Social capital and economic integration of visible minority immigrants in Canada. *Journal of International Migration and Integration, 14*(2), 263–85.

Reich, C., and Zeigler, S. (1972). *A follow up study of special education and special high school students.* Toronto, ON: Toronto Board of Education.

Reich, R. (1992). *The work of nations.* New York, NY: Vintage Books.

Reitz, J.G. (2001). Immigrant skill utilization in the Canadian labour market: Implications of human capital research. *Journal of International Migration and Integration, 2*(3), 347–78.

Reitz, J.G. (2007). Immigrant employment success in Canada: Individual and contextual causes, Part 1. *Journal of International Migration and Integration, 8,* 11–36.

Ritter, J. (1978). *New dimensions for educating vocational education students at the second-ary school level*. (Unpublished Master's thesis). University of Alberta, Edmonton, AB.

Roessingh, H. (2004). Effective high school ESL programs: A synthesis and meta-analysis. *Canadian Modern Language Review, 60*, 611–36.

Rose, M. (2012). Rethinking remedial education and the academic–vocational divide. *Mind, Culture, and Activity, 19*, 1–16.

Rosecrance, R. (1999). *The rise of the virtual state*. New York, NY: Basic Books.

Rosenbaum, J. (2001). *Beyond college for all: Career paths for the forgotten half*. New York, NY: Russell Sage Foundation.

Rosenstock, L., & Steinberg, A. (1999). Vocational education. In M. Apple & J. Beane (Eds), *Democratic schools* (pp. 41–57). Buckingham, UK: Open University Press.

Sadler, L., & Clark, N. (2014). Building community capacity to support Karen refugee youth in schools. In C. Brewer and M. McCabe (Eds), *Immigrant and refugee students in Canada* (pp. 183–201). Edmonton, AB: Brush Education.

Saunders, R. (2008). *Pathways for youth to the labour market: A synthesis report*. (Report prepared for Canadian Policy Research Networks). Ottawa, ON.

Schissel, B., & Wotherspoon, T. (2003). *The legacy of school for Aboriginal people*. Don Mills, ON: Oxford University Press.

Schuetze, H. (2003). Alternative education and training in Canada. In H. Schuetze, & R. Sweet, (Eds), *Integrating school and workplace learning in Canada* (pp. 66–92). Montreal, QC: McGill-Queen's University Press.

Schuetze, H., & Sweet, R. (eds). (2003). *Integrating school and workplace learning in Canada*. Montreal, QC: McGill-Queen's University Press.

Scott, R., Salas, C., & Campbell, B. (2006). *Revisiting NAFTA: Still not working for North America's workers*. Centre for Policy Alternatives. Retrieved from http://www.policy-alternatives.ca/sites/default/files/uploads/publications/National_Office_Pubs/2006/Revisiting_NAFTA.pdf

Scullen, J. (2008). *Women in male dominated trades: It's still a man's world*. Regina, CA: Apprenticeship and Trade Certification Commission.

Seath, J. (1910). *Education for industrial purposes*. (Report prepared for the Ontario Department of Education).

Sedunary, E. (1996). Neither new nor alien to progressive thinking: Interpreting the convergence of radical education and the new vocationalism in Australia. *Journal of Curriculum Studies, 28*(4), 369–96.

Semple, S. (1964). *John Seath's concept of vocational education in the school system of Ontario, 1884–1911*. (Unpublished Master's thesis). University of Toronto, Toronto, ON.

Sennett, R. (2006). *The culture of the new capitalism*. New Haven, CT: Yale University Press.

Sennett, R. (2008). *The craftsman*. New Haven, CT: Yale University Press.

Shavit, Y., & H. Blossfield. (1993). *Persistent inequality: Changing educational attainment in 13 countries*. Boulder, CO: Westview Press.

Shilling, C. (1987). Work-experience as a contradictory practice. *British Journal of Sociology of Education, 8*(4), 407–23.

Simon, R., Dippo, D., & Schenke, A. (1991). *Learning work: A critical pedagogy of work education*. Toronto, ON: OISE Press.

Simon, S. (2015, Jan 9). Federal price tag for Obama's 'free college' proposal: $60 billion. *Politico*. Retrieved from http://www.politico.com//story/2015/01/obama-free-com-munity-college-federal-price-tag-114129.html

Skillbeck, M., Connell, H., Lowe, N., & Tait, K. (1994). *The vocational quest: New directions in education and training*. London, UK: Routledge.

Smaller, H. (2003). Vocational education in Ontario secondary schools: Past, present and future? In H. Schuetze & R. Sweet (Ed.), *Alternation education and training: Preparing for work in the new economy*. Montreal, QC: McGill-Queen's University Press.

Smith, A. (1997). The contribution of the Economic Council of Canada to business economics in Canada. *Canadian Business Economics, 6*, 117–20.

Smith, M. (2001). Technological change, the demand for skills, and the adequacy of their supply. *Canadian Public Policy, 27*(1): 1–22.

Sperling, G. (2007). Rising-tide economics. *Democracy: A journal of ideas, 6*. Retrieved from http://www.democracyjournal.org/6/6547.php

Stamp, R. (1972). Urban industrial change and curriculum reform in early twentieth century Ontario. In R. Heymann, R. Lawson, & R. Stemp (Eds), *Studies in educational change* (pp. 11–87). Toronto, ON: Holt, Rinehart and Winston.

Stanley, T. (2012). White supremacy, Chinese schooling, and school segregation in Victoria: The case of the Chinese students' strike, 1922–23. In S. Burke & P. Milewski, *Schooling in transition* (pp. 237–52). Toronto, ON: University of Toronto Press.

Statistics Canada. (2003). *Characteristics of Canada's newest immigrants*. Retrieved from http://www.statcan.gc.ca/pub/89-611-x/4067689-eng.htm.

Statistics Canada. (2008). *Labour force historical review 2008*. (Report Cat No. 71F0004XCB). Ottawa, ON: Statistics Canada.

Statistics Canada. (2012). Labour force survey estimates (LFS), employees by union coverage, North American Industry Classification System (NAICS), sex and age group, annual (CANSIM Table 282–0078). Ottawa, ON: Statistics Canada. Retrieved from http://www4.hrsdc.gc.ca/.3ndic.1t.4r@-eng.jsp?iid=17

Statistics Canada. (2013, November 25). The education and employment experiences of First Nations people living off reserve, Inuit, and Métis: Selected findings from the 2012 Aboriginal Peoples Survey. *The Daily*. Statistics Canada. Retrieved from http://www.statcan.gc.ca/daily-quotidien/131125/dq131125b-eng.pdf

Stolz, S., & Gonon, P. (2012). Inclusion and exclusion—A challenge in the context of globalisation. In S. Stolz & P. Gonon (Eds), *Challenges and reforms in vocational education: Aspects of inclusion and exclusion* (pp. 9–27). Bern, Switzerland: Peter Lang.

Supiano, B. (2013, April 10). Employers want broadly educated new hires, survey finds. *Chronicle of Higher Education*. Retrieved from http://chronicle.com/article/Employers-Want-Broadly/138453/

Tal, B. (2012, December 13). The haves and have nots of Canada's labour market. *In Focus*. CIBC Economics. Retrieved from http://research.cibcwm.com/economic_public/download/if_2012-1203.pdf

Tal, B. (2013, June 10). Job quality—not what it used to be. *Canadian Employment Quality Index*. CIBC World Market. Retrieved from http://research.cibcwm.com/economic_public/download/eqi-cda-20130610.pdf

Taylor, A. (1997). Education for industrial and "post-industrial" purposes. *Educational Policy, 11*(1): 3–40.

Taylor, A. (2001). *The politics of educational reform in Alberta*. Toronto, ON: University of Toronto Press.

Taylor, A. (2002). In/forming education policy. *Journal of Education Policy, 17*(1), 49–70.

Taylor, A. (2005). "Re-culturing" students and selling futures: School-to-work policy in Ontario. *Journal of Education and Work, 18*(3), 321–340.

Taylor, A. (2006a). "Bright lights" and "twinkies": Career pathways in an education market. *Journal of Education Policy, 21*(1), 35–57.

Taylor, A. (2006b). The challenges of partnership in school–work transition. *Journal of Vocational Education and Training, 58*(3), 319–36.

Taylor, A. (2007). *Pathways for youth to the labour market: An overview of high school initiatives.* Report prepared for Canadian Policy Research Networks. Ottawa, ON.

Taylor, A. (2009). Mapping VET partnerships. *Vocations and Learning, 2*(2), 127–51.

Taylor, A. (2010). The contradictory location of high school apprenticeship in Canada. *Journal of Education Policy, 25*(4), 503– 517.

Taylor, A., & Foster, J. (2015). Migrant workers and the problem of social cohesion in Canada. *Journal of International Migration and Integration, 16*(1), 153–72.

Taylor, A., & Freeman, S. (2011). "Made in the trade": Youth attitudes toward apprenticeship certification. *Journal of Vocational Education and Training, 63*(3), 345–62.

Taylor, A., Friedel, T., & Edge, L. (2009). *Pathways for First Nations and Métis Youth in the Oil Sands.* Report prepared for Canadian Policy Research Networks. Ottawa, ON.

Taylor, A., Friedel, T., & Edge, L. (2010). First Nation and Métis youth in northern Alberta: Toward a more expansive view of transitions. In J. Bruhn (Ed.), *Aboriginal Policy Research Initiative, Policy Research Paper Series.* Ottawa, ON: Institute on Governance. Retrieved from http://iog.ca/publications/first-nation-and-metis-youth-in-northern-alberta-toward-a-more-expansive-view-of-transitions/

Taylor, A., & Krahn, H. (2009). Streaming in/for the new economy. In C. Levine-Rasky (Ed), *Canadian perspectives on the sociology of education* (pp. 103–23), Toronto, ON: Oxford University Press.

Taylor, A., & Lehmann, W. (2002). 'Reinventing' vocational education policy: Pitfalls and possibilities. *Alberta Journal of Educational Research, 48*(2), 139–61.

Taylor, A., Lehmann, W., & Raykov, M. (2014). "Should I stay or should I go?" Exploring high school apprentices' pathways. *Journal of Education and Work.* [advanced online publication]. doi: 10.1080/13639080.2014.887199

Taylor, A., Lehmann, W., Raykov, M., & Hamm, Z. (2013). *High school apprenticeship: Experiences and outcomes.* Report for Ontario Ministry of Training, Colleges and Universities and CAREERS the Next Generation. Edmonton, AB.

Taylor, A., Raykov, M. & Hamm, Z. (2015). The experiences of female youth apprentices in Canada: Just passing through? *Journal of Vocational Education and Training, 67*(1), 93–108.

Taylor, A., Servage, L., & Hamm, Z. (2014). Trades and aides: The gendering of vocational education in rural Alberta. *Journal of Research in Rural Education, 29*(8), 1–15.

Taylor, A., & Spevak, A. (2003, May). Institutionalizing school–work transition in Ontario. Paper presented at the Canadian Society for the Study of Education (Socinet). Halifax, NS.

Taylor, A., & Steinhauer, E. (2010). Evolving constraints and life "choices": Understanding the pathways of students in First Nations communities. In P. Sawchuk & A. Taylor (Eds), *Challenging transitions in learning and work* (pp. 65–84). Rotterdam, Netherlands: Sense.

Taylor, A., & Watt-Malcolm, B. (2007). Expansive learning through high school apprenticeship: Opportunities and limits. *Journal of Education and Work, 20*(1), 27–44.

Taylor, A., & Watt-Malcolm, B. (2008). Building a future for high school students in trades. In D. Livingstone, K. Mirchandani, & P. Sawchuk (Eds), *The future of lifelong learning and work: Critical perspectives* (pp. 217–32). Rotterdam, Netherlands: Sense Publishers.

Taylor, A., Watt-Malcolm, B., & Wimmer, R. (2013). Hybridity in two Canadian provinces: Blurring institutional boundaries. In T. Deissinger, J. Aff, A. Fuller & C.

Jorgensen (Eds), *Hybrid qualifications: Structures and problems in the context of European VET policy* (pp. 165–80). Bern, Switzerland: Peter Lang.

Thiessen, V., & Looker, D. (1999). *Investing in youth: The Nova Scotia school-to-work transition project.* Ottawa, ON: Human Resource Development Canada and Nova Scotia Department of Education and Culture.

Toronto District School Board, The Achievement Gap Taskforce. (2010). The Achievement Gap Taskforce draft report. Toronto, ON: Toronto District School Board. Retrieved from http://www.tdsb.on.ca/Portals/0/Community/Community%20Advisory%20committees/ICAC/Subcommittees/AchievementGapReptDraftMay172010.pdf

Tremblay, D., & LeBot, I. (2003). *The German dual apprenticeship system: Analysis of its evolution and present challenges.* Retrieved from http://www.teluq.uquebec.ca/chairee-cosavoir/pdf/NRC03-04A.pdf

Unwin, L. (2004). Growing beans with Thoreau: Rescuing skills and vocational education from the UK's deficit approach. *Oxford Review of Education, 30*(1), 147–60.

Vadeboncoeur, J., & Collie, R. (2013). Locating social and emotional learning in schooled environments: A Vygotskian perspective on learning as unified. *Mind, Culture, and Activity, 20,* 201–25.

Van Houtte, M., & Stevens, P. (2009). Study involvement of academic and vocational students: Does between-school tracking sharpen the difference? *American Educational Research Journal, 46*(4), 943–73.

Walther, A. (2006). Regimes of youth transitions: Choice, flexibility and security in young people's experiences across different European contexts. *Young: Nordic Journal of Youth Research, 14*(2), 119–39.

Watt, D., & Roessingh, H. (2001). The dynamics of ESL dropout: Plus ça change… *Canadian Modern Language Review, 58,* 203–22.

Watts, A. (1991). The concept of work experience. In A. Millar, A. Watts, & I. Jamieson (Eds), *Rethinking work experience* (pp. 16–38). London, UK: Falmer.

Weis, L. (1990). *Working class without work: High school students in a de-industrializing economy.* New York, NY: Routledge.

Weissman, J. (2012, August 31). Our low-wage recovery: How McJobs have replaced middle class jobs. *The Atlantic.* Retrieved from http://www.theatlantic.com/business/print/2012/08/our-low-wage-recovery-how-mcjobs-have-replaced-middle-class-jobs/261839/

Westheimer, J., & Kahne, J. (2004). What kind of citizen? The politics of educating for democracy. *American Educational Research Journal, 41*(2), 237–69.

Wheelahan, L. (2012). The problem with competency based training. In H. Lauder, M. Young, H. Daniels, M. Balarin, & J. Lowe (Eds), *Educating for the knowledge economy? Critical perspectives* (pp 153–65). London, UK: Routledge.

Willis, P. (1977). *Learning to labour: How working class kids get working class jobs.* Westmead, UK: Saxon House.

Wirth, A. (1974). Philosophical issues in the vocational-liberal studies controversy (1900–1917): John Dewey vs. the social efficiency philosophers. *Studies in Philosophy and Education, 8*(3), 169–82.

Wishart, D., Taylor, A., & Shultz, L. (2006). The construction and production of youth "at risk." *Journal of Education Policy, 21*(3), 291–304.

Wotherspoon, T., & Schissel, B. (2001) The business of placing Canadian children and youth "at risk," *Canadian Journal of Education, 26*(3), 321–39.

Yau, M. (1996). Refugee students in Toronto schools. *Refuge, 15*(5), 9–16.

Young, D. (1992). *An historical survey of vocational education in Canada* (2nd edn). North York, ON: Captus Press.

Young, M. (1998). *The curriculum of the future: From the "new sociology of education" to a critical theory of learning*. London, UK: Falmer.

Young, M. (2003). Durkheim, Vygotsky and the curriculum of the future. *London Review of Education, 1*(2), 99–117.

Young, M. (2010). The future of education in a knowledge society: The radical case for a subject-based curriculum. *Journal of the Pacific Circle Consortium for Education, 22*(1), 21–32.

Index

dual credit projects, 55, 57–8, 63; in Alberta, 60, 61

earnings: apprenticeships and, 101; clerical, 35; non-standard work and, 19–20; unionization and, 22
Economic Council of Canada (ECC), 37, 39, 52
economy: education and, 7–10, 13–28, 29–45; service, 16–19; types of, 47; youth transitions and, 27–28; *see also* knowledge economy
Edmonton: Aboriginal students in, 97–98; VET in, 92–95
Edmonton Journal, 24
Edmonton Public School Board, 92–94
education: barriers to, 82–83; composite, 37; comprehensive, 66–67; critical connective, 113; definition of, 53; dual system of, 84; expectations of, 1, 7–10; industrial, 31–34; linked, 77; market for, 92–94; mismatch with jobs and, 48; role of, 29–45; social policy and, 47; special, 84, 86; technology, 30–31; three E's of, 107; transformation of, 107–109; unified, 77; *see also* vocational education and training (VET)
employer groups, 4, 34, 43–44
employers, 52, 63; in Alberta, 59, 61–62; in Germany, 51; school-to-work initiatives and, 51, 52, 59, 61–62, 63; training and, 25; workplace learning investment and, 49
employment: casual, 20; nature of, 19–21; non-standard, 19–21; v. profession, 67; quality of, 8; service sector, 17–19; youth, 47
English-as-a-second-language: streaming and, 89
ethnicity: streaming and, 89; *see also* race
Europe: education systems in, 1–2; *see also* specific countries
expansive/restrictive training, 80, 93

federal government: in Germany, 51; VET funding and, 36–38
First Nations, 86, 96; *see also* Aboriginal students
First Nations, Métis, and Inuit (FNMI)

students, 96; see also Aboriginal students
"flexicurity," 22
Fort McMurray, AB, 96
Framework for Enhancing Business Involvement in Education, 42–43, 59, 61–62
Fraser Institute, 54
Freeman, S., 45
Fuller, Alison, and Lorna Unwin, 80, 93

Galabuzi, Grace-Edward, 85, 89
Gaskell, J., 84
gender: apprenticeships and, 100–102; commercial education and, 35; school-to-work initiatives and, 62; service economy and, 18; streaming and, 89, 91
"Generation Y," 13
Germany: school-to-work transition in, 49–52; VET programs in, 2, 11, 25–26, 106
Gleeson, Denis, and Ewart Keep, 47, 62–63
globalization, 14–16; unions and, 21
Globe and Mail, 18, 26
Grubb, Norton, 53
Guile, David, 6; and Michael Young, 80–81, 103
Gunderson, Morley, 15

Hager, Paul, and Terry Hyland, 45, 104
Hall-Dennis Report, 38
Hango, D., and P. de Broucker, 48
Harbord Collegiate Institute, 35
Harder Report, 40, 41
Harris, Mike, 54
Hauptschule, 51
Hayward, G., 52
hierarchy, status, 66–70
high schools, 35; as minimum requirement, 44
Hope-Goldthorpe Scale, 67–68
human capital theory, 3, 7, 22–24
hybrid qualifications (HQ), 78
Hyslop-Margison, E., 66

immigrants: labour markets and, 24–25; streaming and, 85
"inclusion," 2